INTERVIEW ANSWERS IN A

FLASH

by

Pat Criscito, CPRW
ProType, Ltd.
Colorado Springs, Colorado

Dee Funkhouser, M.A., M.A.
AB Services, Inc.
Manitou Springs, Colorado

BARRON'S

ACKNOWLEDGMENTS

Thank you to all of the human resource experts who reviewed these questions and answers and provided valuable feedback on today's hiring expectations. They include, in alphabetical order:

Laura Benjamin, Author of <u>The CARLA Concept</u> and National Speaker

Steve G. Carlton, Regional Human Resources Manager, H&R Block

Cindy E. Clark, Director of Human Resources, The Broadmoor Hotel and Resort

Stephen David, Former General Manager, Human Resources, Colorado Springs Utilities

Sandy Dorman, Human Resources Director, Classic Companies

Doug Peden, Executive Director of Human Resources, Falcon School District 49

Anthony Pedilla, Senior Technical Recruiter, Intel Corporation

Richard D. Schur, MS Ed., President and CEO, Up A Notch, Inc.

Christine Virgen, Executive Recruiter, Virgen Consulting

<u>All inquiries should be addressed to:</u>
Barron's Educational Series, Inc.
250 Wireless Boulevard
Hauppauge, New York 11788
www.barronseduc.com

ISBN-13: 987-0-7641-3331-2
ISBN-10: 0-7641-3331-4

PRINTED IN CANADA
9 8 7 6 5 4

INTERVIEW ANSWERS IN A FLASH

Your palms are sweating, your heart is pounding a million miles an hour, and your brain feels like mush! You are sitting in the outer office of a hiring manager, waiting for your first interview in three years. How are you going to present your experience and qualifications in such a way that **you** are the candidate the company chooses?

First, you need to read this book. It won't take long. The book is set up in "sound bite" format so you can quickly find the questions that you know will be the most difficult to answer. You may be asked only 10 or 15 of these 200 questions, but you will never know which ones you will be asked, so you need to be prepared. After you have selected the questions you think will be the biggest challenge for you:

1. Read over the rationale for each question—what is the interviewer looking for; what does he or she expect to hear?

2. Read the sample answer to give you some ideas.

3. Make some notes or write your personal answer to the question in the space provided on each flash card. Keep your answers short. One to three minutes per question is the longest your answer should be. Five minutes would be pushing it, and some questions will take literally only seconds to answer.

4. Tear out the flash cards from the book on the perforated lines and use them to practice your answers over and over again until your responses come naturally.

5. Review the checklists in this chapter to help you be prepared in every way.

Now you are ready to enter that interviewer's office with confidence. No more sweaty palms and pounding heart. Your mind is clear and ready for anything.

What Makes This Book Special?

Research, research, research! We spoke with human resource (HR) managers all across the country (and took many of them to lunch). We asked them to review a list of nearly a thousand questions that commonly appeared in other interview strategy books. They highlighted the questions their companies typically ask and added questions that were not on our list. Then we consolidated all the lists and provided you with the answers to the most difficult questions asked by the vast majority of HR managers.

We were careful to select subject matter experts from a wide variety of industries—Fortune 500 and small to medium organizations in many industries, including manufacturing, retail, service, education, government, and nonprofit, as well as HR consultants. After we prepared our answers to the 200 questions in this book, our experts reviewed those answers to make sure we were on track with typical hiring expectations.

In addition to the 200 "hard" questions we answer in this book, you need to be prepared to answer the "easy" questions that are a part of nearly every interview (e.g., When can you start? What degree did you earn in college? Do you have a driver's license? And the list continues). You don't need our help with these.

What Is the Purpose of a Typical Interview?

Employers want to know:

- Your motivation and personality.
- Your qualifications—skills, education, knowledge, and abilities.
- What benefits you will bring to the company.
- Whether or not you will be worth the money they pay you.
- What you have accomplished in the past that will translate well into this new job.
- Whether or not you will be a good "fit" for the company's culture.

Your answers should concentrate on the employer's needs, not yours. Do your research before the interview and learn all you can about the company, its products, the industry, and the company's competition. In your answers, emphasize how you can help the company achieve its goals. Don't make the interviewer drag accomplishments out of you.

Take responsibility for communicating your strengths. It is the only way your interviewer can determine whether or not you will be worth your salary.

The interview is also your chance to express yourself and to learn more about the company and the opportunity. Always be prepared to ask questions during and at the end of the interview. In the checklist section of this book, you will find a list of possible questions to ask.

Types of Interviews

Every type of interview has its own purpose. Sometimes the purpose is to narrow down the candidates to a smaller pool (as in a screening interview) or to identify real-time specific skill sets (hands-on, competency-based interviews or simulation exercises), or it may be to determine compatibility and social skills (team-on-team) or to see how you handle stress (a panel interview). Other types of interviews are just different because of their format (media-based or during a meal).

- **Screening Interview:** General questions are asked in this type of interview, usually by an HR representative. The screening interview may include questions on self-management, communication, critical thinking, or motivation. It is used to determine basic qualifications and is often done by telephone.

- **Traditional, One-on-One Interview:** This might be your only interview or one of several. A one-on-one interview can be a screening interview, a skills-determination interview, or a final hiring session.

- **Panel Interview:** This is a several-to-one interview, and you're the one! Address your response to the person who asks the question and be prepared for stress.

- **Team-on-Team Interview:** Generally, a work team is looking to replace a lost member and interviews several people at once by interacting with them all.

- **Hands-on (competency-based) Interview:** You've **talked** about what you can do; now the interviewer wants to **see** what you can do. This is an opportunity to demonstrate your skills. Examples might include a typing test, troubleshooting a circuit board, wiring a router, or welding a piece of sheet metal.

- **Simulation Exercises:** These exercises can be a part of almost any type of interview. They often include formal presentations, group exercises, case studies, role playing, and in-box exercises, among other tests of skill.

- **Interviews with a Meal:** This type of interview can be quite stressful. Let everyone else sit first, and use the proper utensils. Don't drink alcohol or order messy foods. Avoid selecting the highest-priced food on the menu—medium-priced items are best. Don't salt your food without tasting it first. Don't talk with your mouth full, and thank your host for the meal.

- **Interviews with a Tour:** On the tour, pay attention to how employees work together, dress, and act. Do they seem happy? Are they smiling? Ask questions about what you see.

- **Internal Candidate Interview:** Prepare for this interview just as you would prepare for any other outside your current company.
- **Media-based, Video- and/or Audio-conferencing:** Be personable. Don't get carried away with hand gestures, but be animated and don't let your voice go into "monotone mode." Avoid stepping out of the camera shot or moving too far away from the speaker.

Games Interviewers Play

In our interviews with hiring and HR managers across the country, we asked for examples of games interviewers might play. These games are sometimes power plays by the interviewer, but usually they are about how you handle stress and distractions. The purpose is often to uncover personality flaws you are trying to hide by being in control of yourself. If the stress or distractions cause you to let down your barriers and reveal your true self, then the interviewer has accomplished his or her goal.

Actually, we recommend that you put up as few barriers as possible anyway. It is better to be yourself, so you can be more relaxed. Successful interviewing is all about being honest and prepared. If you have practiced your answers with the flash cards, then you can be **real**—and the little games interviewers might play won't frustrate you as much.

Examples of some games interviewers have been known to play:

1. Distractions

- Has someone knock on the door to see how you cope.

- Offers coffee or water after the interview has begun.
- Answers e-mails or plays with a PDA, Blackberry, or anything else during the interview.
- Accepts interruptions, like taking phone calls during the interview.
- Leaves the room, returns, leaves again, returns.

2. Stress

- Uses a confrontational interview style.
- Delays the interview, making you wait.
- Rushes through the interview.
- Stares at you long enough to make you uncomfortable.
- Asks trick or torture questions intended to make you nervous.
- Assumes and pushes the negative, and waits for you to correct it. For instance, "What do you do when you work with someone you can't stand?" A correcting response might be "I've been lucky not to experience that yet. However, I know it might happen someday. Just like you can't pick your relatives, you can't pick your coworkers. But that's no excuse for becoming obnoxious myself."

3. Apparent Interviewer Attitudes

You can't control whether your interviewer is having a bad day, how well prepared the interviewer is or is not, or whether or not he or she is basically a good person. What you

can control is your own attitude, and solid preparation can help you cope with these variables. Be as pleasant, positive, and upbeat as you can throughout the interview, regardless of your interviewer's attitude, which might be:

- Bored
- Irritated
- Indifferent.

4. Interview Style

Match your personal style to your interviewer's, whether it is formal or informal/casual. Be careful not to be **too** informal, though.

CHECKLIST

**BEFORE
THE
INTERVIEW**

❑ Complete an honest appraisal of yourself and your expectations (salary, working hours, benefits). Get feedback from people who know you well and will speak frankly with you.

❑ Generate the positive "you" (psych yourself up).

❑ Do your homework.

   ❑ Research the industry, the company, and the job (see Checklist #2).

   ❑ Ask for a job description.

   ❑ Find out who will be interviewing you.

   ❑ Find out what kind of interview it will be (see pages 6–8).

   ❑ Find out how much time you should allow for the interview.

   ❑ If it's a public facility, take a tour of the facility before the interview.

   ❑ Park outside the building and watch people coming and going in both the morning and late afternoon. Are they smiling/happy? What are they wearing?

❑ Use these flash cards to develop answers to common questions and customize them to your history and style.

❑ Practice with friends, with family (teenagers are especially good), in front of a mirror, or on videotape.

❑ Be prepared for any type of interviewer: average "Joe," high-energy overachiever, analytical decision-maker, congenial/friendly manager, or formal executive. Think about how you would approach each kind of person and mirror their behavior to make them more comfortable with you.

❑ Be sure you are prepared for technical questions.

❑ Make sure you can find the company's location and how long it will take to get there in all types of traffic (MapQuest, Google Local, or practice run).

❑ Choose clothing carefully—one step up from how you plan to dress on the job. Make sure all price tags are removed from new clothing. Polish your shoes.

❑ Call potential references, ask their permission, and then prepare them for an interviewer's call. Send them a copy of your résumé.

❑ Change your voice mail greeting if it is not professional.

❑ Call the company the day before the interview to confirm your appointment.

CHECKLIST

RESEARCH THE COMPANY

Where to Look

❑ Company's Web page (financial report, press releases, history, products, etc.).

❑ Industry Web pages, professional organizations, trade magazines, etc.

❑ Do you know anyone who currently works for the company or used to work for them? Ask questions.

❑ Competitor Web pages.

❑ Local newspapers and magazines.

❑ Your local library for print and electronic materials. Find a reference librarian who is familiar with corporate research and career materials.

What to Look For

❑ What are the company's mission, vision, goals, values, and culture? Are you a "fit"?

❑ What are the current and future trends in your industry?

❑ What appears most important on the Web page? That's what is most important to the company.

- ❏ What does the annual report to stockholders tell you? Is the company privately or publicly held? Is the company profitable? How does that compare to previous years? What is projected for growth? How much debt does the company carry?

- ❏ What is the company's history? How long has it been in business?

- ❏ What are the company's primary business units (organizational chart)?

- ❏ How many employees does the company have? Have there been any recent changes in the number of employees?

- ❏ What products or services does the company sell? Which ones are the cash cows?

- ❏ Who are their key partners, customers, and vendors?

- ❏ Who are the company's principal competitors, their products or services?

- ❏ How can your skills help the company? What problems can you solve for them?

- ❏ Is the Web page user friendly? Can you provide any suggestions for improvement?

- ❏ Does the company value community participation? If so, how?

CHECKLIST 3

COPING WITH ANXIETY

❑ Be prepared with company research and interview practice.

❑ Eat and sleep well in the days preceding the interview.

❑ Do what you usually do to relieve stress (exercise, meditate, have a massage, etc.)

❑ Be yourself.

❑ Focus your energy on positive thinking.

❑ Remember to breathe—often and slowly.

❑ Arrive 15 minutes early.

❑ Walk around the outside of the building before going in.

❑ Empty your bladder immediately before the interview.

❑ If dry mouth is a problem, ask for a glass of water before the interview begins.

❑ If you are obviously nervous or make a mistake during the interview, it is okay to say, "Please forgive me. I really want this job, so I'm a bit nervous."

ON THE
DAY OF THE
INTERVIEW

❏ If you have a morning interview, get up an hour earlier than you normally would.

❏ Relax on the drive to the interview. Listen to music that energizes you.

❏ Come to the interview 10–15 minutes early. There may be additional paperwork to complete.

❏ Turn off cell phone, pager, PDA, Blackberry, or anything that will make noise or interrupt you in any way.

❏ Bring a copy of your résumé, a pen, a small notebook, and your appointment book.

❏ Place the items you are carrying in your left hand, leaving the right hand available for a handshake.

❏ Watch what you eat and drink before the interview.

    ❏ Eat a good meal a couple of hours before the interview so your stomach doesn't growl, then brush your teeth.

    ❏ Be careful with caffeine. If you depend on caffeine, then by all means have your usual "dose." On the other hand, if you are sensitive to caffeine and generally avoid it, don't start now. For some people, it can cause nervousness, dry mouth, or frequent trips to the restroom.

- ❑ If you've eaten something smelly, brush your teeth and use a breath freshener.
- ❑ Be careful of the smell of cigarette smoke on your clothes and hair.
- ❑ Watch your behavior from the moment you enter the parking lot.
  - ❑ Drive politely; you never know who you might cut off!
  - ❑ Act as if you are on display at all times—you are.
  - ❑ You might be standing next to your interviewer on the elevator or meet the key decision maker in the lobby.
  - ❑ Be nice to the receptionist/secretary. They are often asked for their opinion after you have left.
- ❑ Be observant—notice:
  - ❑ Signs on the wall.
  - ❑ Posted articles.
  - ❑ Company information on the coffee table.
  - ❑ Personal things on the interviewer's desk.
  - ❑ Anything that can help you establish a connection.

CHECKLIST

5

FIRST IMPRESSIONS

❑ First impressions are important. More often than not, the interviewer will make a snap judgment about you in the first two seconds of your meeting, and it takes a lot to undo that first impression.

❑ Stand quickly when you recognize the interviewer so the person doesn't have to look down at you. This puts you on an equal footing.

❑ Use a firm handshake and smile. Wait for the interviewer to extend his or her hand first.

❑ Wait to sit until the interviewer is seated.

❑ Don't place anything on the interviewer's desk.

❑ Establish a connection by making small talk about commonalities you have discovered by being observant or by using light humor. You must establish rapport with your interviewer quickly and then maintain it throughout the interview. Even if you are the most qualified person for the job, you might not get the offer if you don't "connect" with your interviewer.

❑ Look people in the eye, but make sure you don't stare. Eye contact should be appropriate in length and comfortable for the other person.

❑ Lean forward to demonstrate that you are engaged in the process.

❑ Smile often, but make sure it is at an appropriate time and not just out of nervousness.

❑ Avoid fidgeting, restless movements. Watch swivel chairs!

❑ Don't play with your hair, face, eyes, pen, or anything else.

❑ Don't chew gum, bite your nails, or grind your teeth.

❑ Display courtesy and good manners.

❑ Walk, sit, stand, and speak confidently. Don't slouch.

❑ Avoid crossing your arms across your chest, crossing your legs, or otherwise closing yourself off (defending yourself) from the interviewer.

❑ Men, don't stare at a woman's cleavage.

❑ Men (sorry, but these things really happen!), don't stand up, spread your legs, and hitch up your beltline. The gesture is domineering, especially with a woman interviewer.

❑ Don't brush your clothes or act overly fastidious.

CHECKLIST 6

COMMUNICATION

❑ Start the interview by thanking the employer for the opportunity to interview and express why you are interested in the position.

❑ Use first names.

❑ Treat each interviewer (from HR to the hiring manager) as if he or she is making the hiring decision. Watch your attitude for anything that could be interpreted as condescending, frustrated, impatient, or irritated.

❑ Mirror the communication style of the interviewer—observe and adapt your body language and speaking style. We are attracted to people who are similar to us.

❑ Listen carefully. Read between the lines; look for hidden meaning in questions. Don't allow yourself to be distracted.

❑ Focus on the question, answer what is asked without wandering, and make your key points in your answer.

❑ Don't be afraid to ask for clarification if you don't understand a question.

❑ Be thoughtful. Take a moment to think about a complex question and organize your answer before speaking. If necessary, repeat the interviewer's question to give you time to think about the answer. Don't talk until you are ready. Don't be afraid of silence.

❑ Be truthful. Exaggeration may get you a job but it won't help you keep it!

❑ Be specific—avoid generalizations and provide concrete examples.

❑ Be direct, sincere, and "real." Above all, be yourself. That's what you are selling.

❑ Get the interviewer talking.

    ❑ You get more information.

    ❑ You create good feelings by making a connection with your interviewer.

    ❑ You will be more likely to get the job.

❑ Don't interrupt the interviewer. Wait for a natural break in the conversation.

❑ Talk at a comfortable speed but not too fast.

❑ Enunciate carefully.

❑ Watch your language—no slang, cursing, repetitive phrases (like, you know, uh).

❑ Be aware of how often you use the "I" word. Using "we" shows you value working with others.

❑ Watch for behaviors that indicate your answers are too long or too short. Don't put your interviewer to sleep. Change the pace of your conversation occasionally.

❑ Don't make odd noises with your mouth or lips.

❑ Be animated—use some hand gestures, but don't overdo it. Keep your hands away from your face.

❑ Lean forward—it shows interest and enthusiasm.

❑ Minimize note taking. It slows down the interview process and reduces eye contact. If you feel you must take notes, ask the interviewer's permission first.

❑ Make sure you emphasize your strong points.

❑ Talk about how well you work with others.

❑ End on a positive note.

CHECKLIST

**QUESTIONS
YOU
MIGHT ASK
(pick fewer
than 10)**

Company Organization

❑ What can you tell me about your company's organization... mission/vision/values?

❑ How long have you worked here?

❑ What do you like best about working for your company? Least?

❑ What do you see as your company's single greatest asset?

❑ How would you describe your company's culture?

❑ How has the company changed over the last three years?

The Department

❑ How many employees does the department have?

❑ Has that number changed significantly over the past six months?

❑ Is the department a cost center or profit center?

❑ What impact does this department have on the organization overall?

❑ What business problems keep you awake at night? (for the hiring manager, not HR)

Position for Which You Are Applying

❑ How long has this position been open?

❑ Is this a new position or would I be replacing someone?

❑ Are you ready and able to hire now?

❑ Why is the former employee no longer in this position?

❑ What is the supervisor's name and title?

❑ What does the company consider the most important duties of the position?

❑ What specific skills do I need to succeed in this job?

❑ How will you know if I'm successful in this job? (This is generally a question for the hiring manager and not the HR interviewer.)

❑ Looking down the road several years, what do you see as the key challenges the person in this position will face?

Your Job Search

❑ I would like to follow up with you, as I am very interested in this position. When do you expect to make a decision? May I call you at that time? (Don't become a pest!)

❑ What is the next step in this process?

❑ If you decide to offer me the job, when would I start?

CHECKLIST

**ON YOUR
WAY OUT
OF THE
INTERVIEW**

❏ Thank the interviewer for his or her time.

❏ Encourage the interviewer to call if additional questions arise or if additional materials are needed (work samples, transcripts, references, etc.).

❏ Don't set a deadline for the interviewer to respond.

❏ Don't mention other offers or other interviews.

❏ Get the interviewer's business card. You need the correct spelling of the interviewer's name and title for your thank-you note.

❏ Ask for the job. "I want this job and I hope you will consider me seriously."

❏ Say good-bye with a firm handshake.

❏ Don't rush out of the room like it is on fire!

CHECKLIST

FOLLOWING UP AFTER THE INTERVIEW

❏ Immediately write and mail a thank-you note to each interviewer. Send the message by e-mail and then follow up with a hard copy. If you think of something important after the interview, mention it in the thank-you letter.

❏ Check your phone messages.

❏ Follow up with the employer as agreed.

❏ Respond immediately to any requests for references, samples of work, documentation of education, and so on.

❏ Keep to your usual routine. Don't sit around and wait for the phone to ring.

❏ Continue in your job search.

❏ When the job offer is very detailed or requires relocation, you may request a copy of the offer in writing before accepting the job.

❏ If you aren't offered the job and you have an opportunity to talk with your interviewer, ask:

    ❏ "What was it about the successful candidate that made him or her the ideal choice?"

❑ "Now that you know what I am capable of doing, who else do you know who could use my skills?"

❑ "Please keep me in mind for any other position you feel would be a good match with my qualifications?"

LIST OF INTERVIEW QUESTIONS BY CATEGORY

This list is meant to help you find a question quickly. We have grouped each question by its main type with its corresponding card number. Be sure to notice the subheadings under the card number on each question. If you find a question particularly difficult, you might want to review all of the questions under that subheading so you will be well prepared for the interview.

INTRODUCTION: Why are we here?

1. Tell me about yourself.
2. Where does your boss think you are now?
3. What is the reason you are seeking work now?
4. Why did you leave your last job?
5. How did you learn about this position?
6. Why are you interested in working for our company?
7. How long have you been looking for a job? Why are you still looking for a job? Why haven't you found a job yet?

EDUCATION AND TRAINING: What have you learned?

8. What college did you attend and why?
9. Why are you applying for a job outside of your major?
10. What was your favorite subject in college?
11. What were your least favorite subjects in high school and college?
12. What has been the most difficult training experience you've ever had?
13. How does your grade point average reflect your work ability?
14. What extracurricular activities did you participate in that prepared you for this job?

15. I see you had an internship in this field. What did you learn from it?

16. Name three things you learned in school that could be used on this job.

17. Why didn't you finish college?

18. In the past year, what continuing education, including professional seminars or conferences, have you attended? Who paid for them?

19. What are your plans for continuing your education and training?

WORK BACKGROUND: What have you done?

20. How did you choose to work in this area?

21. What did you like about your last position?

22. What two areas of your last position did you like least?

23. How would you compare the quality of your work to that of others in the same job?

24. How were you evaluated on your last job?

25. Would you recommend your last place of employment to others? Why or why not?

26. In what ways has your last job prepared you to take on greater responsibility?

27. What makes the position for which you are applying different from your last position?

28. How did you help your company increase its sales/profits this year?

29. What is your current salary? (Or, what is your salary history?)

30. You've been out of the job market for the last six years. Please explain that.

31. What has been your biggest disappointment on the job?

32. What were your most important decisions on your last job?

33. What have you learned from the jobs that you have held?

34. What was the best job you ever had, and why?

35. What were the reasons you went to work for your two prior employers?

36. How do you explain the long gaps in your employment history?

37. I see that you have frequently changed jobs. What would make your stay here different? Why have you changed jobs so frequently?

38. Have you ever been fired or asked to resign? Describe the circumstances.

39. What have you learned from the jobs that you have held?

40. Your last job was very different than the ones you had before. Why did you take that job?

41. Can we contact your references or present/former employers? What will they say about you?

42. How does your military experience add to your job skills?

43. What things in your job give you a sense of accomplishment?

44. What do you consider the most significant accomplishment of your entire career?

45. What was the most interesting suggestion or project you initiated?

46. How does recognition or reward for accomplishment affect your work motivation?

47. Describe your favorite boss.

48. Describe the worst boss you ever worked for.

49. How do you handle tension with your boss?

50. How do you like to be managed?

51. What types of people try your patience?

52. What kind of person do you find it easy to work with?

53. What does it take for a team to work together successfully?

54. What experience have you had with sexual harassment? Describe the circumstances.

55. Describe your understanding of sexual harassment.

SKILLS AND COMPETENCIES: What can you do?

56. What are your key skills?

57. What is the most recent skill you have learned?

58. If I remember only one thing about you, what should it be?

59. What skills do you bring to this job that other candidates aren't likely to offer?

60. How do you manage your time on a typical day?

61. With so much e-mail flying back and forth, how do you manage to prevent it from intruding on your work?

62. How do you set priorities?

63. What happens when you get stressed on the job?

64. How do you handle criticism of your work?

65. Our company is quite different from the firms for which you have worked previously. How will you adapt?

66. What communication skills are important in the performance of your job?

67. How do you establish rapport with clients or coworkers?

68. Define customer service.

69. How do you motivate people?

70. How do you like to be managed?

71. How do you make decisions?

72. How do you solve problems?

73. What do you do when you have trouble solving a problem?

74. In this fast-paced environment we need someone who can think on his or her feet. What makes you this person?

75. How do you deal with ambiguity (uncertainty or vagueness)?

76. How do you evaluate the work of others?

77. How do you handle an angry employee?

78. What are some of the things your supervisor did that you disliked?

79. What experiences have you had that prepare you to supervise people who are older and more experienced than you?

80. How would a subordinate describe your leadership style?

81. Describe a leader you admire.

82. How will you get along with a supervisor who is younger than you?

83. How do you think your lack of experience/degree will affect your ability to perform this job?

84. This job carries with it much more responsibility than you've had before. What makes you ready?

85. You appear to be overqualified for this job. What would cause you to take such a position at this time in your career?

PERSONALITY, VALUES, GOALS: Who are you?

86. What can you tell me that I do not already know about you that would make me hire you?

87. What are your greatest strengths?

88. What contribution do you anticipate being able to make to this position?

89. What do your subordinates, coworkers, supervisors, and friends think are your strengths?

90. What is one of your biggest weaknesses on the job? What are some things that you find difficult to do? Why?

91. What might your current boss want to change about your work habits?

92. After six months on the job, what will be the most annoying thing about you?

93. How do you define success?

94. What factors contribute the most to your success on your current job?

95. How do you explain your job successes?

96. Define the word "failure."

97. What is the biggest work-related mistake you've made? What lessons did you learn?

98. What achievements have eluded you?

99. Describe your personality.

100. What personal quality makes you the perfect hire for this position?

101. What are your pet peeves?

102. Do you prefer working as a member of a team or would you rather work alone? Why?

103. Describe how you establish your credibility.

104. What motivates you to put forth your best effort?

105. What two or three things are most important to you in your job?

106. What do you think determines a person's progress in a company?

107. For what would you like to be remembered?

108. How would your last employer describe your work ethic?

109. What have you ever kept or taken from your employer to which you felt entitled?

110. What do you, as an employee, owe your boss and what does your boss owe you?

111. What tips can you bring to us from your previous company?

112. Describe a major goal you have recently set for yourself.

113. Where would you see yourself in five years? (long-range goals)

114. What career or business would you consider if you were starting over again?

115. What skills would you like to develop in this job?

116. Why did you choose this career?

117. What do you hope to be doing two years from now? (short-term goals)

118. Have you ever taken a position that didn't fit into your long-term plan? How did it work out for you?

119. What accomplishments have you made so far in reaching your long-range goals?

120. How do you feel about your career progress to date?

121. What career path interests you within the company?

122. What are your leisure-time activities?

123. What is the best book you've read in the last year? What did you like about it?

BEHAVIORAL/SITUATIONAL QUESTIONS: Can you tell a story?

124. Tell me about a work group you really enjoyed.

125. Tell me about a business need you fulfilled within a group or a committee.

126. Tell me about a time when you persuaded others to take action.

127. Let me describe the work group you would be joining if we hired you. How would you fit in? What would you see as your role as a team member/builder?

128. You have a history of not getting along with a coworker. Your boss has just asked the two of you to work together on a project. What do you do?

129. Describe a time when your customer service skills and diplomacy have been put to the test.

130. You work in the billing department of a large firm. A customer's order was delayed for unknown reasons, and when she called to complain, she was cut off twice. Now she is calling again. How will you handle her phone call?

131. Tell me about your experience in supervision.

132. Tell me how you delegate work effectively.

133. Tell me about a time when you helped in the development of a subordinate.

134. As a supervisor, what do you do when employees working under you don't get along?

135. Tell me about a time when you needed to provide corrective feedback about the job performance of someone you supervised.

136. Describe the circumstances and how you handled firing someone.

137. What would you do if a member of your staff seemed upset about something but you didn't know what the problem was about?

138. Tell me about a typical day at your last job.

139. Give me an example of taking care of business day-to-day but also thinking long range.

140. Tell me about the biggest project you've worked on from start to finish.

141. Tell me about a project in your last job that you really got excited about.

142. Tell me about the last time you found a creative solution to a problem.

143. Give me an example of a time when you had an idea for improvement and how the company was affected.

144. Tell me about a time when you used your fact-finding skills to gain information needed to solve a problem.

145. You have just returned from vacation. Your boss has scheduled an important meeting at 10:00, a large customer has left a message indicating that a problem must be resolved this morning, and the sales department needs a proposal from you by 11:00. How will you respond?

146. Tell me about a time when you had to juggle priorities to meet a deadline.

147. Describe a time when you had to make an unpopular decision or announcement.

148. Tell me about the last time you went over budget.

149. Tell me about one of your projects that failed.

150. Describe a time when you had to persuade someone to accept your point of view. How were you successful?

151. You are working on your business degree at a local college, and you work as a waiter at night to pay your tuition. How could you implement at work what you are learning in class?

152. Tell me about the last time you saved the company money.

153. Describe a specific example of a time when you took the initiative.

HOMEWORK:
What do you know about us?

154. Why do you want to work in this industry?

155. What important trends do you see in our industry?

156. Who are our three major competitors? What advantages do you think they might have over us?

157. What do you know about our company? How did you get that information?

158. What do you think is our organization's strength?

159. What do you think our number one priority should be?

160. What would you do differently if you ran the company?

161. Why do you want to work here?

162. In what specific ways will our company benefit from hiring you?

163. If you had the opportunity to develop a new product or service to add to our line, what would it be?

164. When and how have you seen or used our product(s) or service(s)? What did you like or not like about them?

165. What do you know about the position for which you are applying?

166. Why do you want this job?

167. How is your experience relevant to this job?

168. If you are hired, what do you plan to do in the first week/month on the job?

169. What would you like to accomplish in your first year if we hire you?

170. If you could, what would you change about this position?

JOB FIT: Are you a match?

171. How would you describe your ideal work environment? What environments allow you to be especially effective?

172. Describe your ideal company to work for.

173. If we hire you, what aspect of this job do you think you'll like best?

174. What aspects of this job will you like least?

175. How does the frequent travel required for this job fit into your lifestyle?

176. You don't live in the community where you will be working. How will the commute affect your work?

177. Our company believes that employees should give time back to the community. How do you feel about that?

178. What would you say if I told you that you were giving a poor interview today?

179. I have interviewed several people for this job. Why should I hire you?

180. When would you be available?

181. How flexible are your working hours?

182. Each employee in this department works overtime one weekend a month. How do you feel about that?

183. What do you expect your starting salary to be?

184. The salary you are asking for is near the top of the range for this job. Why should we pay you this much?

185. Why would you consider a cut in pay to take this job?

186. How long would it take to move Pikes Peak?

187. Why are manhole covers round?

ILLEGAL QUESTIONS:
Who would ask these anyway?

188. **AGE**

How old are you?

When were you born?

When did you graduate from high school/college?

Aren't you a little young to be seeking a job with this much responsibility?

Aren't you a little old for a fast-changing company such as ours?

When do you plan to retire?

Are you near retirement age?

189. **HEALTH**

How many days were you sick last year?

Do you have a heart problem?

You are limping. Did you hurt yourself?

Are you physically fit?

How is your health?

Have you ever been denied health coverage?

Are you handicapped? Do you have any disabilities?

Have you ever filed for workers' compensation?

Have you ever been injured on the job?

Do you have a back problem?

How much do you weigh?

When was the last time you saw a doctor?

Do you take prescription medications?

How much money do you spend on prescription drugs?

Have you ever been denied health (or life) insurance?

When was the last time you were in the hospital?

Do you see a doctor regularly?

How many surgeries have you had?

When was the last time you had a physical exam?

Have you ever been treated for a mental health problem?

Have you ever been treated for substance abuse/drug addiction?

Did you get stuck with a lot of medical bills last year?

You need to complete this medical history before we can consider you.

190. MARITAL STATUS

Are you single, married, separated, or divorced?

What's your marital status?

Do you live with your parents or alone?

Does your spouse support your decision to work?

Will your spouse mind the long hours you will be working here?

Will your family be okay with the frequent travel required on this job?

Are you a single parent?

Do you have any children?

Are you planning to have children?

What are your child care arrangements?

Have you ever been married before?

How do you want to be addressed: Mrs. or Miss?

Who is the boss in your family?

Is your spouse employed? Will the fact that both of you work be a problem?

191. RACE/ETHNICITY

What is your nationality/race?

Where were you born?

That's a _____ (Greek, Italian, Spanish) surname, isn't it?

What language do you speak at home?

Where were your parents born?

What kind of accent is that?

Have you served in the military of countries other than the United States?

Can you read English well enough to take this test?

192. CRIME

Have you ever been arrested?

Have you ever committed a crime?

Have you ever pled guilty to a crime?

Have you ever been in jail?

193. RELIGION

Are you (Jewish, Christian, Buddhist,…)?

Are you a member of any religious group?

What church do you belong to?

Do your children go to (Sunday school, church, synagogue,…)?

Will your religion keep you from working on weekends?

Do you sing in the church choir?

What organizations do you belong to?

Is there a religious reason why you didn't shake my hand?

INTRODUCING YOURSELF

Tell me about yourself.

This is a tough question to answer because you don't know for sure what the interviewer is seeking. In general, however, interviewers ask this question for two reasons: 1. to learn more about you and what you consider important than will be obvious from your résumé, and 2. to see how well you are able to think on your feet. Don't simply provide your work and educational history. For small companies, add some personal information—how long you have lived in the area, what the composition of your family is—and end with a statement that relates to the company where you are interviewing. For large organizations, provide a picture of your work persona that goes beyond your résumé.

Answer for a small business: "I moved here about ten years ago and really have enjoyed living is this area. The hiking, skiing, and natural beauty are wonderful. I've been married for five years and have one child who is just starting to hike with my husband and me. We both want to instill a love of the outdoors in her early. Part of the reason I am interested in working for your company is my appreciation for the outdoors. Your company has supported all of the initiatives to create increased park land in our area over the last five years, and I want to work for a company like that."

Answer for a medium-sized company in a city: "I have lived in this area of the country all my life. I love the urban environment, opportunities to participate in the arts, museums, and ethnic restaurants. My family and I try to spend at least one day together each week, visiting local neighborhoods and learning something about their history. One of the reasons I applied for employment with your company is my desire to work for a locally owned company."

Answer for a large corporation: "As you can see from my résumé, I have a lot of experience helping customers solve problems. In my current position, I am responsible for working with approximately 150 families. As a result, I have become highly organized and complete my documentation of service directly after working with a customer. In my last review, I received the highest customer service rating in my group."

Your answer: _____

_____

_____

_____

_____

_____

JOB SEARCH

Where does
your boss think you are now?

Obviously, this answer is going to depend on what you have told your boss about today. The best answer is honest, straightforward, and short. Do not focus on anything that could be perceived as negative.

☞ "I took a vacation day so I could be relaxed and focused on this interview."

☞ "My boss and I have discussed my career opportunities and she has helped me with my decision to look for a new job. My current company cannot offer the advancement I am seeking."

☞ "My lunch hour is flexible so I am currently on break."

Avoid answers such as, "She thinks I am at a doctor's (dentist, school, etc.) appointment." Or, "I took a sick day today."

Your answer: _____

_____

_____

_____

_____

_____

_____

_____

_____

JOB SEARCH

What is the reason you are seeking work now?

There are several reasons for changing employment—a recent job loss, return to work after a period of unemployment, completion of education or training, or a decision to change employment for a better opportunity or advancement, for example. Think about your reason for leaving your most recent employer or why you are choosing to leave your current employer. If your reason could be perceived as negative (i.e., you were in conflict with your boss or you were fired), think about all of the reasons you are choosing to move to a different employer and pick one you can use. Your answer should be both positive and honest.

☞ "I recently left my employer to seek a new position. While my previous company is a good one, I felt that my department was too small to accommodate much advancement for me. When I discussed this issue with my boss, he agreed."

☞ "My last employer overextended financially and, unfortunately for everyone concerned, the result was a layoff. I am now seeking similar employment, with opportunities to learn new skills and make a contribution. I believe your company would be a great match for me."

Your answer: _____

_____

_____

_____

_____

_____

_____

_____

_____

JOB SEARCH

Why did you leave your last job?

Be positive here. Even if, in your heart of hearts, you hated your last job, find something good to say about how it ended. It won't do you any good to whine about it now. Put it behind you and move on. Here are some ideas for good endings.

☞ "Our department was eliminated (or consolidated)."

☞ "My company went out of business (or restructured)."

☞ "I'm interested in more responsibility and growth than my previous employer was able to offer. From my research, it appears that your company is on the cutting edge of our industry and there is room for me to advance."

☞ "I recently earned my bachelor's degree, and I'm ready to move into a supervisory position that can use the education I've worked so hard to complete. My previous employer wasn't able to provide that opportunity."

☞ "I am currently at the top of the salary range for my position. I would like an opportunity for salary growth."

Your answer: _____

_____

_____

_____

_____

_____

_____

_____

JOB SEARCH

How did you learn about this position?

This question may sound like it deserves a simple "I read it in the newspaper" answer, but you really want to demonstrate to the interviewer that you are using a bit more thought in your job search. You aren't just scanning the help wanted ads every Sunday and lounging around the house the rest of the week. Your job search should occupy 20 to 30 hours a week. You want to think of your job search as a marketing campaign that requires a lot of research, networking, advertising, and active searching. Reflect that work in your answer.

☞ "I read the newspaper classified ads every day, so I noticed your account executive opening when it was first listed. I immediately went to your Web site and discovered that your company manufactures several products that I already use. My Internet research turned up a lot of information about your organization. It seems that you have a strong market presence in our region and your products have a proven reputation for reliability. It would be exciting to sell something I like and can recommend with confidence."

Your answer: _____

_____

_____

_____

_____

_____

_____

_____

_____

_____

JOB SEARCH

Why are you interested in working for our company?

Before the interview, you should have done some research on the company where you are interviewing. What caught your attention? What made the company interesting to you, causing you to apply? People like to be proud of where they work and that includes your interviewer. So, you want to be able to say nice things about the company. Is it locally owned or international? How many employees does it have? Is it active in the community? Are its products/services of high quality? What about the company's customer service philosophy, mission, and values?

☞ "I am interested in working for your company because you value our community, and your employees are important to you. You are often in the newspaper, participating in community cleanup activities or contributing volunteer hours to senior citizen events. Your employees speak highly of the company and its products, and they seem very pleased with their jobs. Those qualities in an employer are important to me."

Your answer: _____

_____

_____

_____

_____

_____

_____

_____

_____

_____

_____

7

JOB SEARCH

How long have you been looking for a job? Why are you still looking for a job? Why haven't you found a job yet?

Depending on how long you have been job seeking, you may find this a difficult question to answer. The most important part of your answer is the attitude you have toward your job search. Whether you have been looking for a new job for a short time, a long time, or intermittently, you will want to demonstrate a positive attitude toward your anticipated success in finding the job you want. You can talk about your commitment to finding the job where you feel you can best make a contribution or the job that will make the best use of your skills.

☞ "I have been job seeking for about four months and find that my search is turning up some interesting possibilities. Your position, however, appears to offer the best opportunity for me to make a strong contribution to my employer by using my most well-developed skills. In addition, this position provides me with opportunities to advance and learn new skills. I am very excited about the possibility of working for you."

☞ "I have just begun my job search, so I was very excited to see your advertisement for this position on the Internet. I am interested in the job for two main reasons: the team approach your company is known for, and the opportunity it would afford for me to do what I do best."

Your answer: _____

_____

_____

_____

_____

_____

_____

_____

_____

_____

COLLEGE CHOICE

What college did you attend and why?

The interviewer is trying to gather facts that can be checked easily, so always tell the truth. However, there is an ulterior motive here as well. The interviewer is trying to understand your history and motivations. You will need to develop your own script here, but we can give you some <u>Cliff's Notes</u>. Think: I chose the college because:

☞ It had a good reputation.

☞ It had the types of job-related courses I needed for my career.

☞ It had a competitive atmosphere.

☞ It was close to home and I needed to save on living expenses.

☞ It was out of state and I felt that getting away from home and experiencing a new environment would be good for me.

☞ I knew I wanted to study something in science, and this school had a good science department.

☞ My parents insisted that I attend, but I made the most of the experience and gained a terrific education.

☞ "I went to _____ College/University in _____ (City), _____ (State). I chose that particular school because…"

Your answer: _____

_____

_____

_____

_____

_____

_____

_____

_____

_____

_____

_____

_____

_____

MAJORS

Why are you applying for a job outside of your major?

Think about the job for which you are applying and your college major. How might they be related? What skills or special knowledge did you gain from your college course work that also applies to the job you are seeking? Now expand your thoughts to include other experiences, educational or work-related, that are in any way related to this potential job or are related to your interest in this potential job. Your answer to this question should weave in the information you gleaned from thinking about why you chose this college in the first place.

☞ "Although my degree is in political science and I would be a human resources technician for your company, many of the skills I learned in college apply to this position. For example, my course work taught me to listen to information carefully and draw my own conclusions about its meaning, rather than relying on someone else to make those decisions. My internship in the state legislature required that I gather information on public issues and summarize that information. In addition, I volunteered with an information and referral agency that placed me in contact with people who had a variety of needs. I worked closely with community agencies to identify how those needs might be met. This job would require similar information-gathering and coordination skills. Finally, I am very interested in human resources, so I am highly motivated to put my generalist skills from college to specific use in this job."

Your answer: _____

_____

_____

_____

_____

_____

_____

_____

_____

COURSES

What was your favorite subject in college?

What was your favorite subject and why? (You can't pick recess.) If possible, the subject needs to be a "core" subject such as math, science, English, and social studies, or a technical course directly related to your job performance. What skills or information did you learn in that course that apply to the job you are seeking? That's what you need to talk about as you answer this question.

☞ "I loved my history classes. I learned a great deal about how culture affects the way that people respond to each other and how much our pasts can contribute to our world view. The result has been a more understanding 'me' in the workplace. I think that I am a better team player, a better friend, and a better person as a result of those classes."

☞ "I really enjoyed my science classes. They taught me how to develop an experiment on a small scale before applying a plan or program on a larger scale. Even today, I continue to use the scientific method to solve problems in my workplace."

Your answer: _____

_____

_____

_____

_____

_____

_____

_____

_____

_____

_____

COURSES

What were your least favorite subjects in high school and college?

Before you answer this question, think about the courses you have taken that could apply to the job for which you have applied. Those are the course examples you **do not** want to use to answer this question. What other courses did you take? You might choose a required course, one that you thought would be good and wasn't, or some course that got on your schedule because of the time slot. You are safest choosing an elective rather than a core subject.

☞ "Probably one of my worst classroom experiences occurred during my sophomore year of college. It was a geology course on the American Southwest and required a huge amount of memorization without a lot of independent thinking, questioning, or discussion. Unfortunately, I think part of my dislike for this course was based on the instructor's apparent disinterest in the class. It was a pretty basic course and she seemed more interested in getting through it than whether or not we learned the information being presented."

Your answer: _____

_____

_____

_____

_____

_____

_____

_____

_____

_____

COURSES

What has been the most difficult training experience you've ever had?

Think about all of your education and training experiences to date. Some of these experiences may have been formal (college or high school course work, seminars, workshops), while others could have been informal (on-the-job training, self-taught information). Make sure to include information about why the education or training experience was difficult and the ultimate result of the training.

☞ "In college, I took a French course that I was really excited about. From the first day of class, the instructor wanted us to speak only French whenever we were in the classroom and wouldn't let us see the written words. Pronunciation was hard and understanding the words spoken to me was even harder. I began to feel totally stupid and dreaded going to the class. Finally, I realized that I am a visual learner and needed to see the words on paper to retain them. I talked to the instructor about my problem and she accommodated my learning style. It really improved my ability to retain what she was teaching."

☞ "In my last position, I attended a two-day workshop on the implementation of a new computer software program designed to increase tracking of business results. While the system turned out to be wonderful, the trainer for these two days was difficult to understand. He used no visual materials, had no handouts, often went on tangents with the information, and was not available to answer additional questions over the breaks or lunches. After the training, I realized that I would have to work with the new system on my own to become competent using it. Once I spent a couple of hours working with the software, I was able to assist coworkers as well."

Your answer: _____

_____

_____

_____

_____

GRADES

How does your grade point average reflect your work ability?

The reality is that grades by themselves are not always a clear indicator of performance on the job. If you begin your answer by apologizing for your grades, it can indicate that your self-esteem or confidence in your abilities is low. Regardless of your GPA, you will want to take responsibility for what you achieved; think about how your study habits could reflect positive work behaviors on the job. In addition, you could talk about anything that is different about your life in the work world versus your life as a student.

☞ "My grade point average in college was not something to be proud of, although I did manage to get my degree and I am proud of what I learned. As I'm seeking employment now, I have thought about what will be different between my school and job performance. While attending school, I worked part-time at night and lived at home with my parents so I could help to take care of my younger sister while both of my parents worked. As soon as I begin to work, I plan to get my own apartment and focus on learning my new job."

Your answer: _____

_____

_____

_____

_____

_____

_____

_____

_____

_____

14
PREPARATION FOR THE JOB

What extracurricular activities did you participate in that prepared you for this job?

The last five words of this question are the key to a correct answer. As with most interview questions, the answer should be related to what you learned that can benefit your new employer. If you are going for a sports marketing job, your personal sports interests become important. If you are looking for a management job, your experiences that developed leadership skills should be your focus. If you will be part of a team, communication and teamwork are number one. If you are applying for a job with a nonprofit organization, any fund-raising would be key. If you want an internship in Washington, DC, your participation in political science clubs and campus elections would be valuable.

Avoid saying, "I was working so hard on my studies that I didn't have time for extracurricular activities." This won't impress your future boss, who wants a more well-rounded employee. One of the problems with today's prevalent distance learning and colleges centered on providing education to working adults is that these institutions rarely provide opportunities for school-sponsored extracurricular activities. That means you will have to pull examples from your volunteer work in the community.

☞ "As a member of the Political Science Club at the University of Denver for two years, I was selected as the college's Election Commissioner and helped to coordinate the voting process on campus for the 2004 elections. I was one of the key factors in a three-fold increase in voter turnout, which set a record for the university. Because of my participation in the club, I won an internship with the Assistant Minority Leader in the Colorado legislature in 2004, where I gained valuable research, communication, campaign, and writing skills that would be true assets in your Legislative Assistant position."

Your answer: _____

_____

_____

_____

_____

_____

_____

_____

_____

PREPARATION FOR THE JOB

I see you had an internship in this field. What did you learn from it?

Your internship should have given you an opportunity to apply the various concepts you learned in school to a work environment. Review the company information and job description. How is the company with which you completed your internship similar to the company from which you are seeking employment? How about the similarities between the internship job and the job for which you are applying? Now compose your answer by talking about what you learned in your internship as it applies to the job you want.

☞ "My internship was with a governmental agency that had begun providing new services to businesses. I got a lot of experience explaining the benefits of those services to a variety of small and large companies and then delivering services to meet the results of a company needs assessment. I was successful in my efforts and enjoyed the work. In this position with your company, I would be providing business-to-business services based on an informal needs assessment. I look forward to the opportunity to meet with your clients and help them address their needs with our products."

Your answer: _____

_____

_____

_____

_____

_____

_____

_____

_____

16

PREPARATION FOR THE JOB

Name three things you learned in school that could be used on this job.

Think about the primary lessons you learned in school. In addition to specific subject matter, you learned some technical skills and some work behavior skills. Which of these skills could be important to your performance on this job?

☞ "I graduated from college cum laude; my success in school was directly related to my work habits. I learned how to plan my schoolwork and then work that plan. I feel confident in my ability to successfully meet deadlines, work on group projects, and produce timely reports. All of those skills will be assets in this job."

Your answer: _____

_____

_____

_____

_____

_____

_____

_____

_____

_____

_____

17
DROPOUT/DELAY

Why didn't you finish college?

This is a very sensitive question for a lot of people. Sometimes people feel inadequate because they don't measure up to society's (or their own) expectations. A degree is becoming more and more important in today's business world, and it is often a key hiring qualification. However, many times experience can be substituted for a degree, so don't beat yourself up when you answer this question. There are plenty of acceptable reasons for dropping out of school.

☞ "I had to leave school for financial reasons. My parents couldn't afford my tuition, so I chose to go to work instead. I gained some valuable experience and maturity that prepared me to succeed in college now that I'm an adult. I'm looking forward to finding a distance-learning program that I can complete while I work."

☞ "It took me a while to find my direction. I enrolled in college right out of high school, and I didn't know what I wanted to do with my life. I drifted from one major to another, and to be honest, I wasn't getting very good grades. I dropped out after the first year and went to work in our local bank. I was selected for an internship and discovered that I really enjoyed accounting. Since then, I've enrolled in night classes to finish my education. I intend to go on to get an MBA in finance."

Your answer: _____

_____

_____

_____

_____

_____

_____

_____

_____

_____

LIFELONG LEARNING/STAYING CURRENT

In the past year, what continuing education, including professional seminars or conferences, have you attended? Who paid for them?

Education doesn't end when you finish high school or college. It is a lifelong process. The half-life of a college degree today is three to five years. That means if you're not retooling or gaining new knowledge, your education can become obsolete very quickly, especially in the sciences, health, and technology. Those who are committed to continuing education are more likely to move ahead in their careers, boost their earning power, and make their skills more marketable. They will have the competitive edge so necessary in today's cutthroat markets. It is no longer possible to take a job right out of high school, be trained by an employer, and work for the same company until retirement. There is no gold watch at the end of the rainbow, and this trend is unlikely to change. Your interviewer wants to make sure you understand these trends and are committed to lifelong learning. As for who paid for your classes, it's okay if your employer paid for them, but it's even better if you financed them yourself. It shows a real commitment to personal growth.

☞ "Since I finished my bachelor's degree, I've taken two graduate courses at Regis University. Because I travel so much, I've been researching online MBA programs, and I think I've found one that will let me study at my own pace and still provide me with a quality education. My current employer doesn't pay for education, so I am going to get a college loan to help finance my MBA."

☞ "I love learning new things! In the past year, I've taken two communication and employee supervision seminars, which were sponsored by my company, and I took the initiative to attend a weekend Fred Pryor workshop on time management, which I paid for myself. In addition to formal training, I am a voracious reader. My favorite book this year has to be <u>Good to Great</u>, which helped me understand how a company can succeed by staying committed to its core competency."

Your answer: _____

_____

_____

_____

_____

_____

_____

_____

_____

_____

LIFELONG LEARNING/STAYING CURRENT

What are your plans for continuing your education and training?

The primary reasons we continue our education is because we want to stay current with new information in our field of work and to develop new skills. These points are exactly what you want to talk about when answering this question. Think about your current goals. What additional education or training will you need to reach those goals? Your answer could be that you plan to attend a seminar to develop a particular skill or gain an additional certification, that you will take advantage of up-to-date training in your industry through your membership in a professional or trade organization, or that you plan to return to school over the next couple of years to complete an advanced degree. Whatever formal or informal plans you have will provide your answer to this question.

☞ "Since I just graduated from college, I really want to concentrate on learning my job at this point. I made some great contacts in school, however, and joined a couple of professional organizations. That way, I can get new information about our field and industry through their publications and seminars. Long term, I plan to go back to school for a master's degree."

☞ "So much is constantly changing in our industry that I find it very important to attend seminars as they become available, and I read trade publications. Right now, those are my primary avenues for continuing my education. As I identify new skills that could be important to my job performance, I will attend additional training to obtain those skills."

Your answer: _____

_____

_____

_____

_____

_____

_____

_____

_____

_____

_____

20
PRESENT JOB

How did you choose to work in this area?

What drew you to your career area? Was it training in a specific field or a general education with work experience? Often, we see ourselves as "falling into a job"; however, there's a reason for staying in that job or that field, and that is what the interviewer is looking for with this question. Your answer may tell the interviewer how goal oriented you are and how willing you have been to take charge of your career.

☞ "When I completed a degree in mass communication at Kansas State University, I thought about what my first real job might look like. While I was in high school, I worked in retail sales and really loved those jobs, so I decided that I would apply my degree in that same direction. I began looking for opportunities in sales with products I already knew. That actually is what got me interested in your company and why I am here today."

Your answer: _____

_____

_____

_____

_____

_____

_____

_____

_____

_____

_____

PRESENT JOB

What did you like about your last position?

Ideally, you will be able to identify something from your last job that you particularly liked (and did well) and that you will also be doing in this job. If you can't come up with a job duty that you would perform in both jobs, think about a duty in your previous job that used the same skills you would use in this job.

☞ "My last job required a lot of coordination between members of our team as well as members of a client company team. Before this experience, I had no idea how easy it would be to miscommunicate with so many people! I learned the importance of checking back with others regularly to make sure I understood my duties. Regular meetings of the entire team also helped to keep us all on track. In your company's position, I would be dependent on the work of other team members in much the same way. Because my experience in the last job was so positive, I really look forward to developing relationships and working closely with a team again."

Your answer: _____

_____

_____

_____

_____

_____

_____

_____

_____

_____

_____

PRESENT JOB

What two areas of your last position did you like least?

This question can be tricky to answer. You want to be honest, so first you will need to think about the two areas in your previous job that you liked least. Now, think about the job for which you are applying. Is either of those two "liked least" components going to show up on the new job? If so, see if you can think of another area for your "liked least" answer. For example, did you like working independently, or with a team? Maybe you would like a different mix of independent and team work. Other "liked least" areas could be working in a "cubicle forest," too much or too little travel, not being able to see the results of your work, having to complete redundant paperwork, too much routine or change, or not being able to establish a balance between home and work, among others.

Remember to frame your answer as positively as possible, even though you are providing negative information. The interviewer is asking this question to get a better feel for who you are.

☞ "I really liked my last job, so this is a tough question for me to answer. I suppose that one of the things I didn't appreciate about my last job was the cubicle environment. While I have worked in cubicles before, this environment seemed particularly noisy and it was hard for me to concentrate on my work. Secondly, our work was undergoing constant change as contract expectations changed. While I appreciated the variety of work I got to perform, I rarely got any feedback about the quality of that work, so it was hard to know what I could improve."

Your answer: _____

_____

_____

_____

_____

_____

_____

_____

_____

_____

23

PRESENT JOB

How would you compare the quality of your work to that of others in the same job?

To respond to this question, you will want to talk about the high quality of your work without putting someone else's work down. Think about the quality of the work you perform. What can you say about it? What have previous supervisors or coworkers said about your work products?

☞ "The quality of the work I perform is excellent and that impression is supported by performance evaluations I've received from previous supervisors. When I supervise others, I've been told that I have high expectations for their work performance, and I certainly apply that standard to my own work as well. When working on a team, I am often the identified 'go to' person when someone needs an answer to a question, so I am able to contribute to the quality of my coworkers' job products as well."

Your answer: _____

_____

_____

_____

_____

_____

_____

_____

_____

_____

_____

PRESENT JOB

How were you evaluated on your last job?

The answer to this question could be a discussion of an annual evaluation, a quarterly or semi-annual discussion between you and your supervisor, a coaching relationship with identified timelines and specific outcomes, or an informal "attaboy" without formal evaluation. In the latter example, the company for which you worked may not have had an evaluation system at all, taking the attitude that if you weren't fired, you were doing fine! What is important about this question is that you demonstrate that you take responsibility for your own job performance and that you welcome assessment of your progress.

☞ "Our evaluation system was designed with both formal and informal components. I was evaluated after the first six months on my job, and then annually for the five years I worked for the company. Before each evaluation, I received a copy of the form my supervisor completed. I was asked to provide any feedback I was interested in sharing and to develop performance goals for the coming year. When the performance evaluation session was held, my supervisor would review last year's goals, provide me with feedback, request my input, and together we would develop next year's goals. While no other formal meetings were scheduled, I knew my supervisor was available if I wanted help reaching my goals. I also knew that I was expected to regularly challenge myself to reach the annual goals we set."

Your answer: _____

_____

_____

_____

_____

_____

_____

_____

_____

_____

PRESENT JOB

Would you recommend your last place of employment to others? Why or why not?

Whether you liked your previous employer or not, you need to answer this question in a positive manner. Identify one or two reasons you could use to recommend your previous employer to others. These points may be characteristics of your previous employer that did not work well for you. For example, the company may be highly predictable, causing you to feel that the work was too routine. This same characteristic may be positive for someone else. Other examples include: the company is always seeking new talent for its management ranks (rather than promoting from within); it is constantly changing the way tasks are accomplished (without promoting a sense of consistency); the company has high expectations for all of its employees (rather than recognizing all contributions, including small ones). If you liked your previous employer, this question will be easier to answer.

☞ "I would recommend my former employer to others. Company XYZ was a wonderful place to work. I enjoyed the people with whom I worked, the environment was pleasant, and the work expectations from my supervisor were attainable. Unfortunately, there was nowhere for me to advance or I would still be working there."

Your answer: _____

_____

_____

_____

_____

_____

_____

_____

_____

_____

_____

26
PRESENT JOB

In what ways has your last job prepared you to take on greater responsibility?

Think about some part of your last job that gave you the opportunity to learn a new skill, practice a new process, or work with others in a new way. Any of those examples could help you to answer this question. Next you want to think about how the new duties or experiences helped you to take on more responsibilities.

☞ "My last job was really a pivotal position for me. While I have supervised employees in the past, I had never been responsible for an entire department. In addition to supervising thirty people instead of ten, I was responsible for running a budget, meeting departmental deadlines, improving the work flow, and managing our department's relationships with other departments across the state. I now feel ready to take on this job with confidence."

☞ "My current job has really given me an appreciation for the importance of documenting work and meeting deadlines. While I have had to do some documentation in every one of my jobs, this position required closer attention to detail. As a result, my documentation has been helpful to the continuous improvement process in our plant, and my opportunities for promotion increased."

Your answer: _____

_____

_____

_____

_____

_____

_____

_____

_____

_____

PRESENT JOB

What makes the position for which you are applying different from your last position?

In the job for which you are applying, will you be accepting more responsibility or learning new information? Will this position make better use of your skills or teach you new skills? If your response to any of the above is "yes," you have just identified your answer to this question.

☞ "While the work I would be performing for you is substantially the same as in my previous position, I will be supervising five employees here. That is one of the characteristics of this job that really appeals to me. I have done a little supervision in the past, but only to fill in for other supervisors who were on vacation or out of the office for a period of time. I really look forward to supervising my own team and implementing some of the skills I learned in my college management classes and from observing others."

Your answer: _____

_____

_____

_____

_____

_____

_____

_____

_____

_____

PRESENT JOB

How did you help your company increase its sales/profits this year?

Interviewers are always looking for ways to determine whether or not you will be worth your pay. This question is one of those ways. If you increased sales or profits for your current employer, then you will be more likely to do the same in the new job. It is all about making money or saving money and/or time for your employer.

For a sales representative: "I consistently exceeded sales quotas every month, which contributed $150,000 more to my company's bottom line last year alone."

For a PR person: "I created and implemented a promotional plan for a beauty salon, which resulted in the client being listed as one of the top 200 salons nationwide in <u>SALON Today</u> magazine."

For a marketing manager: "I developed and implemented marketing programs that grew Lucent's enterprise wireless business from zero at startup to $30+ million annually."

For a secretary or clerk: "I created a comprehensive filing system so information was well organized and easily retrievable. This saved the department 20 hours a month."

For a production manager: "I increased productivity 5 percent by relocating inventory on the production line more efficiently. The new method made it easier to package orders by placing the most frequently used items in a central location."

Your answer: _____

_____

_____

_____

_____

_____

_____

PRESENT JOB

What is your current salary? (Or, what is your salary history?)

The one who mentions dollars first loses! Don't play the game. Avoid answering this question as long as you possibly can. You want the interviewer to talk salary numbers first. Long before you are in this hot seat, you should have done your homework on the Internet to determine what the average salary is for this position and how your pay will be affected by the cost of living in the area. If you are moving from Boise, Idaho, to the Silicon Valley, your salary history is truly irrelevant. You and the interviewer will have to calculate a considerable raise to cover the increased cost of California living. To figure out what your salary should be (or should have been), you can turn to the Internet for help (**www.patcriscito.com** and select "career resources"). There are two basic types of salary sites on the Internet. One is based on salary surveys of various industries—the average salary for your type of job without figuring the cost of living into the equation. The other is a cost-of-living calculator—you made this much "here" and would need to make so much "there" to make up the difference. To answer this question, there are several comebacks that will throw the ball back into the interviewer's court.

☞ "While salary is important to me, other considerations—including benefits, vacation time, and the opportunity to learn new skills—are also important. I would like to have the salary discussion when I move to the next stage of this process."

☞ "I think it's premature to talk about salary just yet. I haven't had time to give you enough of my history so you can put my salary into context. I would rather talk about my experience and accomplishments first. I'm sure we can come to some agreement when you're ready to offer me the job."

☞ "I'm sure you need that information at some point in order to make your decision about hiring me, and I would be happy to provide you with it, but right now I would rather wait until you are closer to making me an offer."

If the interviewer just won't continue with the interview until you have answered the question, then you have no choice but to cooperate. In that case, provide a range and not a single number. It will give you some "wiggle" room later in the negotiation.

☞ "I made from $_____ to $_____ on my last job. However, my employer was a small start-up company and couldn't afford to pay me the going rate in our industry. I accepted the job anyway because I was excited about the challenge of building a business from the ground up. I found the job very rewarding."

Your answer: _____

_____

_____

_____

PRESENT JOB

You've been out of the job market for the last six years. Please explain that.

Your potential employer is concerned about your ability to return to work successfully at this time or this question would not be asked. Returning to work after an extensive absence requires a total shift in lifestyle and you want to reassure the interviewer that you are prepared to make this change. In addition, the interviewer needs to know what you have done to maintain awareness of the changes in your field.

☞ "I worked full time after college graduation until the birth of my first child. I returned to work after his birth; however, when he turned one, I decided to stay home until he was ready for school. During this time, I continued to participate in two professional organizations and read about changes in my profession on a regular basis. My son is now enrolled in school and I am ready to give an employer my full attention again."

☞ "I left my job six years ago to be able to travel extensively with my spouse. Although that was a wonderful experience, I began to miss the stimulation of work after a relatively short period of time. To compensate, I have taken a number of online, postgraduate courses and had the opportunity to attend several seminars in my profession. As a result, I have stayed current and feel ready to return to full-time work now."

Your answer: _____

_____

_____

_____

_____

_____

_____

_____

PAST JOBS

What has been your biggest disappointment on the job?

Disappointment is not the same as failure or weakness, so don't answer this question like you would the failure/weakness questions. Instead, think about how something in your work failed to meet your expectations, which is the definition of disappointment. It would be easy to focus on something negative about the company or the people you worked with. Instead, put as positive a spin on your answer as possible, focusing on what you have learned.

☞ "My biggest disappointment came when I left my job as a sales representative with XYZ Company. I had developed extensive community contacts through networking in various organizations. Some of those contacts were warm leads that I turned over to my replacement. I spoke with a colleague a few months after I left and discovered that my replacement hadn't converted a single lead into a sale. I was disappointed because I had worked so hard to develop those contacts and nothing was gained from my work. Even though I was disappointed, I wouldn't change what I did. I learned that I can't control the actions of other people, so I won't be as disappointed next time."

Your answer: _____

_____

_____

_____

_____

_____

_____

_____

_____

_____

PAST JOBS

What were your most important decisions on your last job?

Regardless of whether you are a queen bee or a worker bee, you make decisions every day. Decisions are not limited to managers. Even at the lowest levels of the organizational chart, all of us decide whether to show up for work on time. We decide to do our jobs well—or not. We decide what tone of voice we will use with colleagues, supervisors, and customers. We decide whether to get the project finished by the deadline—or not. At higher levels, supervisors must decide where to delegate responsibilities, how much money to spend, what types of goals to set, and whether or not to hire or fire an employee.

How you choose to answer this question will tell the interviewer what level of authority you had on your last job and whether you take responsibility for your actions. The key is to select examples of "important" decisions that will be similar to the decisions you will be required to make if you accept the job offer.

☞ "As an event coordinator, I decided where events would be held, what types of entertainment and food would be available, and how to promote the event. The theme was generally decided by the marketing department, but I did decide on the agenda and speakers."

☞ "In my role as an administrative assistant, I made decisions every day for my boss. I managed his calendar and made instant decisions to add or delete meetings from his schedule. I decided which calls to put through to his phone, regardless of his schedule, and which calls could wait."

☞ "During the past two years, I have been working as a call center supervisor. I had to make spur-of-the-moment decisions about how to handle difficult customer calls, how to smooth ruffled feathers, and how many people needed to be trained every quarter."

Your answer: _____

_____

_____

_____

_____

_____

_____

_____

_____

PAST JOBS

What have you learned from the jobs that you have held?

This needs to be something you have learned from previous jobs that you will be able to use in the new job, should you be hired. It could be a skill, some special pieces of information that apply to this industry and company, or a way of doing your work that has been successful for you.

☞ "While I have learned a great deal about my profession in previous jobs, the most critical skills I have developed are about self-management. My first job taught me a lot about time management—how to anticipate and meet work project deadlines. My last job required that I supervise employees, and I found that to be a whole new skill set."

Your answer: _____

_____

_____

_____

_____

_____

_____

_____

_____

_____

_____

PAST JOBS

What was the best job you ever had, and why?

When you answer this question you will want to think about the job for which you are applying. The more "best job" components you state in your answer that are also components of the new job, the better.

☞ "When I worked for ABC Company, I really enjoyed the teamwork required. I looked forward to completing my individual work and presenting the results to my team members. When we ran into difficulties, it was exciting to work together to solve problems. One of the things that caused me to apply for your job is your emphasis on teamwork."

☞ "I've enjoyed part of every job I've had throughout my career; however, my position with XYZ Company was probably my favorite. I am particularly skilled at problem-solving, and that job allowed me to spend the majority of my time solving problems. I was able to work all over the plant with a variety of people at all levels of the organization. The job was fulfilling, intellectually stimulating, and fun! I see many of the same opportunities in the job with your company, which is why I am so interested in this job."

Your answer: _____

_____

_____

_____

_____

_____

_____

_____

_____

35

PAST JOBS

What were the reasons you went to work for your two prior employers?

Your interviewer wants to catch a glimpse of your motives. Do you care about the company's core mission? Do you have a passion for the product or industry? Or are you more worried about the benefits and salary? Are you interested in continued learning and personal growth? Or are you just looking for a way to put bread on the table? Your answer will shed some light on what truly motivates you, but you want to be careful to focus on what matters most to your potential employer. Remember, it's all about being worth your paycheck.

☞ "I couldn't afford to go to college full time, so I had to find a job right out of high school. I didn't want to take just any job, though. It was important to me that I contribute something of value. I knew that I could only do that if I could get some training while on the job. I was fortunate to find an entry-level job with MNO Company because they have a policy of promoting from within, and they helped pay for both technical training and college classes. I took advantage of every class that was offered and worked my way up from an administrative assistant to a production supervisor over three years. Then their industry suffered a downturn and I was laid off. Now that I had some experience, I looked for a company where I could make a difference. My next job allowed me to use the expertise I gained at MNO to increase production on their assembly line by 9 percent the first year and 15 percent the second year. At the same time, I completed my bachelor's degree in business management, and now I'm ready to contribute on a management level."

Your answer: _____

_____

_____

_____

_____

_____

_____

_____

PAST JOBS

How do you explain the long gaps in your employment history?

This is sometimes a tough question to answer, especially if you spent time between jobs watching television. Long gaps without work are often assumed to be a lack of motivation, even if you had a good reason. You need to convince your interviewer that any problem is in the past or that you had an acceptable explanation for the gap(s). Taking time off to be with your children, to care for a sick family member, or for maternity leave is considered acceptable. So is going back to school, traveling abroad, or settling in after a move, but be careful about extended unemployment between jobs because you couldn't find a new job. Your answer should be as brief as possible, because it is very easy to say something here that would leave a negative impression.

☞ "When I was downsized from ABC Corporation, it was just after the dot-com crisis. I knew it would be difficult to find a job making the same salary, so I decided to go back to school and get my Microsoft .NET certification before looking for a new job. I had saved enough money to finance this time off, and it was definitely worth it. The knowledge and skills I gained in school will be a true asset in the job you are offering."

Another answer might be:

☞ "When I left my last job, my wife had just started working from home and she needed a private office. To accomplish that, we needed to add a room onto our house. Because I have experience in construction, we decided it would be less expensive if I built the addition myself instead of hiring a contractor. That's how I spent those three months before looking for my next job. I learned a lot about project management and budgeting with limited resources. It was a great experience that will be valuable to my future employer."

Your answer: _____

_____

_____

_____

_____

_____

_____

PAST JOBS

I see that you have frequently changed jobs. What would make your stay here different? Why have you changed jobs so frequently?

<u>Communication World</u> magazine calls job hoppers "hummingbirds" because they flutter from job to job. Hummingbirds are often younger workers who haven't settled into a career yet, but they can also be experienced workers who are the victim of frequent downsizing or have changed jobs to advance in their profession. This doesn't change the fact that the hiring process is expensive. Companies want to make sure that you will stick around if they hire you, so you need to convince the interviewer that you (or your situation) have changed.

☞ "I have had a number of different jobs, so I understand your question. Part of my changing jobs early in my career was the result of my search for the perfect job. I didn't like either of the first two positions I held. I also didn't do any research on those companies or jobs before I accepted them. I really enjoyed the third job, and as you can see from my résumé, I stayed until that company moved its operation overseas. However, I really learned my lesson about researching companies before accepting job offers. Based on my research and conversations with people who work here, your company reminds me very much of my last employer. The job is very similar as well, which is why I really want to work here."

☞ "As an IT project manager, I have changed jobs about every two years for the past six. I found better opportunity for advancement, increased options for new skills development, and improved salary by this pattern of job change. I'm now in a position where I've purchased a home and started a family, so I intend to be in my next position for a long time."

Your answer: _____

_____

_____

_____

_____

_____

_____

_____

PAST JOBS

Have you ever been fired or asked to resign? Describe the circumstances.

If you have never been fired or asked to resign, this question is easy to answer. If, however, you **have** had that experience, you need to take responsibility for your behavior and explain what you learned from the experience.

☞ "I have always left jobs by resigning without pressure, so this is an experience I haven't had."

☞ "Early in my career I worked for a supervisor with whom I experienced great difficulty. After several attempts to contribute to the work group and resolve my supervisor's concerns, she suggested that I resign my position and I did. What I learned from that experience was the importance of my relationship with my immediate supervisor. Now, when I get a new supervisor, I know to ask questions about her expectations for my performance and to check in regularly to answer questions and maintain communication. Although I have worked directly for several supervisors since that time, I have never again been involved in a conflict. I have learned how to 'manage up.'"

Your answer: _____

_____

_____

_____

_____

_____

_____

_____

_____

_____

PAST JOBS

What have you learned from the jobs that you have held?

Be specific in your answer and relate what you have learned in the past to the new job for which you are interviewing. Avoid talking about what was in it for you, personally. Potential employers want to know what's in it for them. Your answer is all about predicting your future success by evaluating your past experiences.

Customer service: "In my past jobs, I learned a lot about dealing with customers and keeping them satisfied. When I started my first customer service job, I had never worked directly with customers, so I had a lot to learn about managing my tone of voice, especially with unhappy customers. I learned to be patient and to listen empathetically. In my most recent job, my employer gave me a lot of decision-making freedom when it came to keeping customers happy. I learned how to use good judgment in making compromise offers that were truly win-win solutions."

Computer programmer: "When I graduated from college, I had the academic preparation for my first software development job, but I quickly discovered that I had a lot to learn about business in general. You have to understand the context in which your software will be used before you can develop a program that truly meets the user's requirements. I asked for a mentor from management who could introduce me to the entire business. After a year under her wing, I felt much more qualified to design workable solutions."

Your answer: _____

_____

_____

_____

_____

_____

_____

_____

_____

PAST JOBS

Your last job was very different than the ones you had before. Why did you take that job?

First, think about the job this company has to offer. Is it more like your last job or more like the jobs you had previously? Your answer should reflect your interest in the job you are applying for. Next, think about the job or career change you made into your last job. Were there similar skills needed, but in a different environment? Were the differences between previous jobs and your last job exciting to you and therefore you made the change to learn new skills or information? These points can help you craft your response to this question.

☞ "My last job was very different from others I have held, and I appreciated the opportunity to learn new skills. Working for MCI required that I communicate with team members all over the world. I learned a lot about working with people from different cultures and even more about how to develop relationships with people I never got the chance to meet in person. I also improved my attention-to-detail skills by having to read the materials my team members created, rather than listening to them explain all of their reasoning up front. The job was a great experience, but I missed working in a smaller office where I could see the results of my contribution to the company. That is why I have applied for your opening."

Your answer: _____

_____

_____

_____

_____

_____

_____

_____

_____

_____

PAST JOBS

Can we contact your references or present/former employers? What will they say about you?

Can you imagine an employer offering you a job if you answered "no" to this question? Of course you want to provide references, but it should be on your terms. It's okay to answer "no" to a request to contact your current employer, but you want to give the interviewer access to former supervisors, customers, and coworkers who can talk about how you work. Forget friends and family as references, unless an advertisement requests "personal" references. Ask your potential references for permission before listing them. You want to make sure each of them has a copy of your résumé and an idea of the types of jobs for which you are searching. If you are uncertain whether someone will give you a good reference, don't select him or her.

Now, for the second half of the question. Of course you don't know exactly what your references will say about you, but you can be fairly certain that they will be more objective than you are. Before answering this question, you should evaluate your strengths and weaknesses and be brutally honest with yourself. Focus on the positive in your answer, and if you admit to a weakness, either put a positive spin on it or make sure it isn't a critical strength required in the new job.

☞ "Yes, you can contact both my references and former employers. My current employer, however, doesn't know I'm job seeking, so I'd prefer that you keep my search confidential until after you have made a firm job offer and I have given notice."

☞ "What will my references say about me? Well, I hope they will say that I'm a hard worker with a strong sense of integrity. They should give you positive comments about my technical skills and ability to manage team members. If they have anything negative to say, it will probably be about my drive. I tend to work long hours when we are on a tight deadline, and I drive myself and my team pretty hard, although I have to admit we have a good time while we're doing it. I recognize and reward the work of my subordinates after the project is done."

Your answer: _____

_____

_____

_____

_____

_____

MILITARY

How does your military experience add to your job skills?

Even if your military job was loading bombs (which doesn't exactly translate well into the civilian sector), there is something in your military experience that will relate to almost any job. Military training and experience is all about discipline, self-control, leadership, communication, and hard work. If you were lucky enough to work in a field directly related to the civilian sector, then you can talk about concrete skills that will transfer. You don't have to answer questions about your discharge (honorable or otherwise), since interviewers aren't allowed to ask those questions.

☞ "I can bring to you my experience in supervising and evaluating ten subordinates, scheduling projects, and managing an inventory of 200,000 parts in the shop. I was responsible for more than $1.5 million in assets and was commended during inspections for my high-quality accountability systems. This experience makes me highly qualified to serve as a crew chief on your flight line."

☞ "During the past year, I served in Iraq when my Army National Guard unit was activated. As a sergeant, I have gained significant leadership abilities that would transfer well to your Office Manager position. I was accountable for a squad of eleven soldiers, and every one of them made it home safely under my leadership. I know how to motivate others to do their best, and I have a very strong work ethic."

Your answer: _____

_____

_____

_____

_____

_____

_____

_____

_____

_____

ACCOMPLISHMENTS

What things in your job give you a sense of accomplishment?

This question gives you an opportunity to demonstrate your self-awareness. An accomplishment is the result of your action(s). Think about a specific experience when you really felt you made a contribution: a leadership role on a project, an award you won, a problem you solved, or something you created, such as a new system for tracking information. Make an overall statement about your accomplishment that would be important from an employer's perspective and then give a specific example.

☞ "I get a great sense of accomplishment from exceeding expectations. In my last job, I was able to increase product sales by 15 percent in my first year. I remember one of our customers who doubled her orders over that year. She told us that our increased emphasis on providing product information had helped her expand her business. It was a real win-win experience."

☞ "I get a sense of accomplishment from organizing things and developing systems that make work easier. My last employer had difficulty finding things when he needed them. He could spend a lot of time looking for papers, information, or particular files, and became more frustrated by the moment. I developed a filing system that made it easier for him to put things away in a more logical order when he was finished with them, making it easier for him to find them the next time. We even rearranged his furniture to make his files more accessible to him."

Your answer: _____

_____

_____

_____

_____

_____

_____

_____

_____

_____

44
ACCOMPLISHMENTS

What do you consider the most significant accomplishment of your entire career?

Think over your past work and educational experiences. You want to consider accomplishments from your recent past, if possible, so look at your most recent experiences first. Separate duties and responsibilities from specific tasks or projects that you were able to complete successfully (accomplishments). For example, being an excellent supervisor requires a skill set. Improving team relationships resulting in a 10 percent improvement in production is an accomplishment. You can find your successes in a number of areas. Have you been able to increase services, reduce costs, improve product performance, increase sales, reduce waste, or save time? Another place to find accomplishments is in problems you have solved. Where have you improved a customer service system, purchased a new tool to help maintain information, fixed a product or service delivery system problem, or improved employee morale? The three most important points for listing accomplishments are: (1) don't undersell yourself, (2) be realistic in your statements, and (3) be specific about your accomplishment.

☞ "When I went to work for my last employer, employee morale was at an all-time low. Customer orders were being mixed up with the wrong orders going to the wrong customers, and no one seemed to understand why. As a result, providing customer service consisted mostly of listening to complaints, promising to do better, and hoping the next order went out correctly. I began my job by talking with several employees about what they thought was happening in the ordering process and what was going wrong. By combining all of their feedback, it seemed apparent that employees did not understand what they, individually, were responsible for and that no one was being held accountable for anything. Mapping out the ordering process so everyone could see where orders began, and following through to how they were shipped, helped everyone understand the production process. Then it was possible to help all the employees understand their individual responsibilities and hold them accountable. Order accuracy improved by 42 percent, customer service measured by surveys went up by 30 percent, and employee morale increased to such an extent that turnover decreased by 15 percent, all within one year."

Your answer: _____

_____

_____

_____

_____

_____

_____

_____

ACCOMPLISHMENTS

What was the most interesting suggestion or project you initiated?

To answer this question, you want to think of a project or suggestion you initiated that will showcase some of your skills that could be important to the job for which you are applying. Have you recommended a change to the way customer service is provided by your company? Have you made a suggestion to solve a problem? Maybe your main contribution to the company was a suggestion about a choice of software, a change in employee benefits, Christmas party plans, or the purchase of a new tool or machine.

☞ "My last employer was a small company that had been in existence for many years. Billing on accounts, maintenance of customer records, and accounts receivables were all done manually. It took so much time to accomplish anything! I did some research and had a software salesperson come out to talk with the owners about an electronic solution to our problems. The owners were very impressed. I got a bonus for my efforts and the number of mistakes in record keeping was significantly reduced."

Your answer: _____

_____

_____

_____

_____

_____

_____

_____

_____

_____

_____

_____

ACCOMPLISHMENTS

How does recognition or reward for accomplishment affect your work motivation?

While we all appreciate recognition and rewards, some of us need them more than others. Recognition can affect employees in several ways:

☞ Helps define excellence in work.

☞ Gives credit for a job well done.

☞ Is often public, so others can recognize the accomplishment.

☞ Directs the employee to continue producing at a high level.

☞ Creates an attachment between employee and employer.

These types of recognition positively affect employee motivation through external means. External rewards that motivate employees can be as diverse as the employees themselves. Some examples of rewards include money, time off, gift certificates, or new opportunities on the job. Most employees are internally motivated by their need to feel a sense of contribution and accomplishment in their jobs.

☞ "I am highly motivated by my desire to make a contribution to the lives of others. That certainly has affected my choice of employers and the work I have trained to do. In addition, knowing that my employer appreciates my efforts pushes me to accomplish the best in my work."

☞ "As an extrovert, contact with people is really important to me. I love working with clients to improve their products. I am motivated to do my best work by both financial incentives and new opportunities."

Your answer: _____

_____

_____

_____

_____

_____

_____

_____

_____

_____

_____

BOSS/SUPERVISOR

Describe your favorite boss.

What this question is really asking is what is important to you in a supervisor. Is it that your supervisor is fair and sympathetic to your needs—or is a "hands off" approach from a supervisor who is available when you need help most important to you? Do you appreciate being able to work with a boss who treats you as an equal and is willing to get his or her hands dirty and do the work with you? Do you work best with someone who assigns projects and provides a timeline with a check-in schedule, leaving how to accomplish the work to your judgment? Remember that the person to whom you are speaking may be your next supervisor, so think about anything you have learned about this person during your interview so far.

☞ "One of my previous supervisors was so easy for me to work for that I really came to understand how important a skilled boss is to me. She was careful to assign projects with all the information I needed to get started, listened to my concerns when work didn't go as we had anticipated, and was helpful to me as I worked to grow my own skills. As a result, I think I did some of the best work I have ever produced for that company."

Your answer: _____

_____

_____

_____

_____

_____

_____

_____

_____

_____

_____

BOSS/SUPERVISOR

Describe the worst boss you ever worked for.

First, don't name names. You want to show discretion. Second, you really do have to answer this negative question, but try to restrain your criticism. Third, don't let any lingering feelings of resentment creep into your answer. Fourth, try to be as positive as possible, keep your answer short, and quickly turn your answer into what you learned. Fifth, realize that anything you say will give your interviewer insight into how you like to be managed.

☞ "I prefer to focus on people's strengths and not their weaknesses, so this is a difficult question for me to answer. I've been really lucky to work with great people throughout my career. However, I did have a boss one time who had less than admirable ethics. She was a good manager in many ways, but when she asked me to lie to a client, I had to refuse. After the problem was resolved, I asked her for a private meeting to discuss our ethics. My boss and I came to an understanding that we would just have to agree to disagree. I learned that I can't change other people, but it was still important for me to communicate."

Your answer: _____

_____

_____

_____

_____

_____

_____

_____

_____

_____

_____

BOSS/SUPERVISOR

How do you handle tension with your boss?

The best way to handle tension with a boss is to avoid it in the first place. However, we all know that tension occurs on occasion, even within good relationships. Think about the last time you experienced tension in your relationship with your boss. Start by identifying a specific incident that created that tension, rather than trying to explain an overall tense relationship. What was the source of the tension? How did it get started? What was the effect on the relationship? How did it get resolved?

☞ "On my last job, my supervisor and I generally got along well. On occasion, though, I would start a project that had been assigned to me and develop it in a way that was significantly different from my boss's method for managing a project. That would create tension for me and, as I later learned, for him as well. After a couple of negative encounters with my boss, I discovered that I needed to communicate project progress more regularly with him, and it was helpful if I could give him an idea of how I planned to accomplish project goals. That way, we were both clear about what I was doing and he was no longer worried about whether or not I would complete projects on time and on budget. The result was a very positive working relationship."

Your answer: _____

_____

_____

_____

_____

_____

_____

_____

_____

_____

BOSS/SUPERVISOR

How do you like to be managed?

By asking this question, the interviewer is probably trying to determine your "fit" with an existing supervisor. What do you need from a supervisor in order to do your best work? What does your work style require?

☞ "I get very focused on my job tasks, so I really appreciate a supervisor who is willing to schedule a time to meet with me on a regular basis. This prevents the 'drop in' kind of meetings that are not conducive to accomplishing my best work. I appreciate a supervisor who gives me work to be done and then lets me decide how to do it. I also appreciate knowing the supervisor's expectations for my performance when a project is assigned, so I can work to meet those expectations."

Your answer: _____

_____

_____

_____

_____

_____

_____

_____

_____

_____

_____

INTERPERSONAL RELATIONSHIPS

What types of people try your patience?

Always start and finish with a positive, if at all possible. Begin by reassuring the interviewer that you are able to get along with others and then pick a quality in others that you have difficulty working with. As with any negatively focused question, end with your "fix" to the problem.

☞ "I can get along with most people very easily. I like working with others, but I know that, at times, cooperative work can be difficult. I also know that I don't have to like all of my coworkers, but I do need to be able to get along with each of them. The people I probably have to work the hardest to get along with are those who have trouble with flexibility. Whether it's a new way of doing things, a different project, a new person to work with, or simply another task that's being assigned, I would rather work with someone who is willing to try things out than one who wants everything to stay the same. What I have learned through experience is that most people will flex to new opportunities, if the opportunity is presented well. That has caused me to work on how I present information to others, so I am able to get the best results."

Your answer: _____

_____

_____

_____

_____

_____

_____

_____

52

INTERPERSONAL RELATIONSHIPS

What kind of person do you find it easy to work with?

The interviewer is trying to determine whether or not you will "fit" within the work group if you are offered the job. We all have a tendency to relate to people who have traits similar to our own, so whatever traits you choose for this answer are probably going to be a reflection of your own strengths. Select traits that relate to your work and not to your personal life.

☞ "I really enjoy working with people who pull their own weight and do the best work possible. It permits collaboration toward a mutual goal without having to worry about the quality of the end product."

☞ "I find that working with people who have skills that I don't have, or who think differently than I do, challenges me to be more creative. When I collaborate with these types of people, I am energized and the group ends up with some really great ideas."

Your answer: _____

_____

_____

_____

_____

_____

_____

_____

_____

_____

_____

_____

INTERPERSONAL RELATIONSHIPS

What does it take for a team to work together successfully?

Think about the experiences you have had working with teams in previous jobs. What processes and procedures were important to the team's functioning? What can you identify about your team work experiences that made one team successful and another team unsuccessful? Was the team set up differently? Were team members willing and able to work together?

☞ "First and foremost, team members have to be willing to work as a team. Without a commitment to share the work to be accomplished, a team cannot be successful. Secondly, a communication process needs to be in place. How much of that communication needs to be formal and how much can be left to informal communication may depend on the team members' experience working together in the past, but both processes must be present to assist the team in successful completion of the work to be performed. A clear goal, timeline, and defined expectations for the team can also be important."

Your answer: _____

SEXUAL HARASSMENT

What experience have you had with sexual harassment? Describe the circumstances.

Be careful with your answer to this question if you have had any experience with sexual harassment. The best policy is to answer the question honestly, providing as few details as possible. Most important, tell about what you learned.

☞ "Although I have no direct personal experience, I have attended several workshops on sexual harassment and understand the concept. The most important thing to remember, I think, is that sexual harassment is in the 'eye of the beholder' and can occur between members of the opposite or same sex."

☞ "While working for a previous employer, I was subjected to sexual harassment. My employer really seemed to understand the problem and was supportive of me by helping to get the behavior stopped."

☞ "Unfortunately, I was accused of sexual harassment a number of years ago. It was a difficult experience for me but I worked with my employer to resolve the situation. I continued to work in the same department with the same coworkers without any further problem."

Your answer: _____

_____

_____

_____

_____

_____

_____

_____

SEXUAL HARASSMENT

Describe your understanding of sexual harassment.

According to the U.S. Equal Employment Opportunity Commission (**www.eeoc.gov**), sexual harassment is a form of sex discrimination that violates Title VII of the Civil Rights Act of 1964. "Unwelcome sexual advances, requests for sexual favors, and other verbal or physical conduct of a sexual nature constitutes sexual harassment when submission to or rejection of this conduct explicitly or implicitly affects an individual's employment, unreasonably interferes with an individual's work performance or creates an intimidating, hostile or offensive work environment." What we need to remember about sexual harassment is that its occurrence is in the "eye of the beholder." So, even if you do not see a behavior as offensive or hostile, the person on the receiving end of that behavior may see things differently.

☞ "I understand that sexual harassment is any behavior or action of a sexual nature that interferes with another's work or creates a negative environment. I also know that each of us needs to pay attention to our own behaviors, in case they become offensive to someone else. Do you have a specific policy about sexual harassment at this company?"

Your answer: _____

_____

_____

_____

_____

_____

_____

_____

_____

_____

_____

_____

KEY SKILLS

What are your key skills?

Begin by thinking about the skills that are most important to the job for which you are applying. Look at the job description, identify the duties, and list the skills necessary to perform those duties. Now compose a paragraph using those skills.

☞ "One of the things that interests me about this job is the opportunity to use so many of the skills I have developed over my career. This position requires that I work well on a team, and I have excellent communication skills I have found useful in teamwork in the past. In addition, my technical skills with your software are highly developed, and I am comfortable developing presentations for leadership as well as customers. The position also supervises five people. In my last position I supervised several staff members and was able to coach them to improved performance."

Your answer: _____

_____

_____

_____

_____

_____

_____

_____

_____

KEY SKILLS

What is the most recent skill you have learned?

Your answer to this question will reveal how current your skills are, how much you value lifelong learning, and how well qualified you are for the position. A skill can be a strength, but not all strengths are "skills." A skill is more about dexterity, the ability to become adept at a task, than it is about knowledge or personality traits. For instance, typing 90 words per minute is a skill. Being a hard worker is a trait, not a skill. Choose a skill that is critical to your success in the new job. Be honest. Make sure you actually have the skill that you say you do; the interviewer may ask you to demonstrate it.

☞ "I took a night class to learn Microsoft Access at New Horizons about six months ago. I picked it up really quickly and aced the final exam. I noticed in your advertisement that database skills are an important part of this job. Are you using Access or Oracle? Both programs use the same basic processes, so I can easily use either software."

Your answer: _____

_____

_____

_____

_____

_____

_____

_____

_____

_____

_____

KEY SKILLS

If I remember only one thing about you, what should it be?

Relate your answer to the job requirements. If you are seeking a job in customer service, you will want to pick one of your strengths that make you great at communicating with others. If you are looking for a computer programming job, you will highlight your strongest technical skills. If you want a management or supervisory position, then your answer will focus on your ability to lead others. If it is difficult to extract a key skill from the job requirements, answer instead with something about your personality that makes you a valuable employee.

☞ "I want you to remember that I am a terrific team player. I collaborate well with others and appreciate diversity."

☞ "I want you to remember that I have the ability to listen empathetically, which makes me great at customer service, especially in a call center environment."

☞ "I want you to remember that I graduated at the head of my class in network administration. I am on the cutting edge of today's technology, which means I can provide you with the most innovative solutions with little downtime."

☞ "I want you to remember that I led my division to generate the highest revenue and net profit in the company's history."

Your answer: _____

_____

_____

_____

_____

_____

_____

_____

_____

KEY SKILLS

What skills do you bring to this job that other candidates aren't likely to offer?

Think outside the box. Don't rehash your résumé or talk about the typical traits that everyone mentions—strong communication skills, team player, hard worker, etc. This is your chance to really stand out. Make sure the interviewer remembers YOU!

☞ "I was mentored by one of the best salesmen in our industry. He taught me that the best way to win the contract is to provide the WOW Factor… that little something extra that the competition didn't think to do. That's why I have exceeded my sales quotas by more than 150 percent every month for 12 consecutive months without fail. It is precisely that skill that will make you money and that makes me the best candidate for this job."

☞ "I noticed that you recently opened a branch office in Madrid. My grandfather emigrated from Spain and we grew up speaking Spanish in our home. I am fully bilingual in both English and Spanish, and I've traveled often to Spain with my family. I'm familiar with the culture as well. With my MBA from Thunderbird, I could step into the Madrid operation and be immediately useful."

Your answer: _____

_____

_____

_____

_____

_____

_____

_____

_____

SELF-MANAGEMENT: STRESS, TIME, CRITICISM, CHANGE

How do you manage your time on a typical day?

Again, think about what the job will require in terms of time management. Will you be handling multiple duties simultaneously? For example, will you be required to answer a multiline telephone, greet customers coming into the business, take calls from the staff in the office, file paperwork, etc., all at the same time? Will you be working with several customers at once? Will you be assigned to a single project with deadlines you have to meet? The time management skills will be different based on the expectations of the job.

☞ "Time management turned out to be one of the most important skill sets I didn't learn in college. On my first job, I constantly felt 'under the gun' with changing deadlines and projects that grew without notice. I learned quickly that I needed a way to successfully manage my time if I wanted to keep my job. I did some reading on the subject and followed the advice I was given. Now, I am careful to put current projects in the file cabinet next to my desk. I review my schedule regularly to make sure I get to all of my appointments, and I maintain a project whiteboard behind my desk to make sure I'm making the progress needed to meet my deadlines."

☞ "I have a lot of experience managing multiple duties simultaneously. What I find most important is my ability to maintain my cool during times of high stress. Since the customers in our office often dictate my time, the best I can do is to stay calm and remember that everything will get done. If I do run behind on a project, I will talk with my supervisor to get assistance."

Your answer: _____

_____

_____

_____

_____

_____

_____

_____

SELF-MANAGEMENT: STRESS, TIME, CRITICISM, CHANGE

With so much e-mail flying back and forth, how do you manage to prevent it from intruding on your work?

E-mail has increased our accessibility to each other and can take a lot of time to address. It is, however, important to both answer your e-mail and focus on your project, so you will answer this question as a simple problem-solving experience.

☞ "I usually go through my e-mail, voice mail, and snail mail first thing in the morning. I often respond to those messages that are important and will file all others in folders to be addressed later during the day. That leaves the rest of my morning to focus on my project. After lunch, I will return to my e-mail and voice mail, responding as needed. My afternoon is again focused on the project. I will, as possible, review my e-mail again at the end of the day. If you, as my supervisor, feel that I need to review my e-mail more regularly, I would be happy to schedule my time to meet that need."

Your answer: _____

_____

_____

_____

_____

_____

_____

_____

_____

_____

_____

_____

SELF-MANAGEMENT: STRESS, TIME, CRITICISM, CHANGE

How do you set priorities?

Priority setting is a specific skill, so you will need to come up with a plan for setting priorities and be willing to adjust priorities to meet the organization's needs. Most of us set priorities without thinking about them. This question will require that you now make your process for setting priorities concrete. One method that you might use is Covey's process for determining whether a task is important, urgent, both, or none of the above. This method, along with some others, should be easy to research online or in print.

☞ "I find it important to set priorities and then review them regularly. New duties or tasks can change my priorities, so I need to remain clear on when work is due and make sure that I don't get overwhelmed. Generally, I decide what work I have that is considered of high importance to my supervisor and work on that task first. Next I look at deadlines for work projects and plan each project to meet those deadlines. I find MS Project software helpful in maintaining awareness of deadlines approaching. This way, I can make sure that my work is completed on time, with my supervisor's priorities addressed first."

Your answer: _____

_____

_____

_____

_____

_____

_____

_____

_____

_____

_____

_____

_____

SELF-MANAGEMENT: STRESS, TIME, CRITICISM, CHANGE

What happens when you get stressed on the job?

Talk about a loaded question! None of us are at our best when highly stressed. Come up with a stress behavior you exhibit and how you overcome that behavior. Try to put a positive spin on it by talking about how you have learned to cope with that stress behavior.

☞ "When I am stressed, I begin to talk faster, make more gestures, and just move faster. I notice that, when I speed up, the people around me become more stressed and less able to help me with my tasks. As a result, I have taught myself to be aware of how rapidly I am speaking or moving at any given time, and then I can take a deep breath and slow down."

Your answer: _____

_____

_____

_____

_____

_____

_____

_____

_____

_____

_____

_____

SELF-MANAGEMENT: STRESS, TIME, CRITICISM, CHANGE

How do you handle criticism of your work?

This can be a difficult question to answer. None of us like to hear negative comments about our work. When answering this question, you want to talk about criticism you have received in the past, how you responded to that criticism, what you learned from that experience, and what changes in behavior you made as a result.

☞ "In one of my first jobs, I had a supervisor who prized honesty above all other qualities. She was liberal with both her criticism and her praise. One time, she really hurt my feelings by bluntly telling me what I had done wrong when setting up the employee schedules for the following week. She complained about my scheduling, communication, and follow-up. I remember going home thinking about quitting my job after that, but I knew that I needed to come back the next day with a plan for improving my performance in this area.

"The next morning, I met with my boss and went over my plan for changing the way I would schedule employees in the future. My boss asked a lot of questions and made it clear that she liked my plan. Since that time, I have focused on listening to and accepting critical comments about my work. As a result, I am able to incorporate improvements in my work behavior that I might otherwise have avoided."

Your answer: _____

_____

_____

_____

_____

_____

_____

_____

_____

SELF-MANAGEMENT: STRESS, TIME, CRITICISM, CHANGE

Our company is quite different from the firms for which you have worked previously. How will you adapt?

This employer is concerned about your ability to adapt quickly, so you want to be able to address that concern. When in previous jobs have you had to adapt to changing circumstances or tasks? When have you had to learn a new task or new information? How did you adapt to those changes? You may want to provide an example.

Next you want to mention any similarities in skills, values, tasks, or products/services that will help your interviewer see that, although you are changing companies, you understand the work that is to be completed.

☞ "Adapting to change is one of the skills I learned on my previous job where projects constantly changed. While your firm does have a different set of products and is a younger firm than those I have worked for in the past, your mission statement indicates that you hold the same corporate values that were held by my previous company. You want to deliver your products in a cost-effective manner that provides excellent products with high-quality customer service. I share those values, which is why I am interested in working for you."

Your answer: _____

_____

_____

_____

_____

_____

_____

_____

_____

_____

INTERPERSONAL SKILLS/CUSTOMER SERVICE

What communication skills are important in the performance of your job?

All communication skills are important in work environments. In fact, in survey after survey, employers rate communication, problem solving, and teamwork as critical skills every employee needs. Consider all forms and modes of communication commonly used at work in your answer to this question. For example, your verbal, listening, and written skills—as well as face-to-face, telephone, e-mail, report or letter writing modes of communication—need to be included in your answer.

☞ "I find that my job often hinges on my ability to communicate with my coworkers, supervisors, and customers, so I consider communication a critical part of my job. As a team member, my listening and verbal communication skills are important on a daily basis. My ability to pay attention to the body language and facial expressions of others has always helped me understand their expectations of me and the effectiveness of my communication efforts with them. Strong writing skills are necessary as well if I am to document my work performance. While I may prefer face-to-face communication, letters, memos, progress reports, and e-mail can all be effective methods of communicating."

Your answer: _____

_____

_____

_____

_____

_____

_____

_____

_____

_____

_____

INTERPERSONAL SKILLS/CUSTOMER SERVICE

How do you establish rapport with clients or coworkers?

When you meet a new person, how do you conduct yourself? Generally, you are polite, ask questions of each other, and listen carefully to the responses, finding commonalities that help you "connect." That is generally how you begin to develop rapport.

☞ "I am comfortable meeting and working with a wide variety of people; developing rapport in that first couple of contacts is really important to the success of our long-term relationship. I always begin by being pleasant and welcoming, while paying attention to the other person's body language, in addition to listening to what is being said. I ask questions to make sure I understand the information we are exchanging, and make sure to keep all my attention focused on the person with whom I am interacting. As a result, I rarely experience the kind of miscommunication that can occur in new relationships and find that my time concentrating on rapport development is more than worth the effort."

Your answer: _____

_____

_____

_____

_____

_____

_____

_____

_____

_____

INTERPERSONAL SKILLS/CUSTOMER SERVICE

Define customer service.

This question takes some research. If the company you are interviewing has a Web page, brochure, or company report you can review, you can often find information about the company's orientation to customer service, and that's what you need to know to answer this question. Although the question is "define customer service," your answer should define **high-quality** customer service.

☞ "High-quality customer service requires meeting the customer's needs to the best of my ability. To accomplish that, it is important that I first really listen to the customer and repeat the request to make sure I understand the customer's expectations. Then I need to provide what is being requested, get assistance if necessary, or be able to help the customer understand why it can't be done. I think it's very important that the customer knows I am listening and have done everything possible to help."

Your answer: _____

_____

_____

_____

_____

_____

_____

_____

_____

_____

INTERPERSONAL SKILLS/CUSTOMER SERVICE

How do you motivate people?

This is an important question if your job will include any supervision or project management. Job performance is a combination of ability and motivation. Sometimes, the person with the best skills isn't sufficiently motivated to be successful, just as someone without the necessary skills is less likely to be the best choice for hire. Contrary to popular belief, motivation can be taught. Your answer to this question should acknowledge that motivating employees is part of any supervisory or managerial position, and should include some specific ways you have motivated others in the past. The sample answer that follows may provide you with some ideas.

☞ "As a manager, I have always considered motivating employees a significant part of my work. When I begin to work with a new group, I often begin by meeting individually with my employees to ask them about their expectations of me. I take that information and build motivation and performance review plans based on their needs—and on my need to have them perform well. In general, I can then motivate employees by using positive reinforcement, effective discipline, satisfying individual needs, setting appropriate work goals, rewarding positive job performance, and treating everyone fairly."

Your answer: _____

_____

_____

_____

_____

_____

_____

_____

_____

_____

_____

_____

70

INTERPERSONAL SKILLS/CUSTOMER SERVICE

How do you like to be managed?

Think about a really good supervisor you had in the past. If you have not had that experience yet, think about the kind of supervisor you would like to work for. Do you like the security of someone who monitors your progress, giving specific directions? Do you prefer being given a project and then checking in at identified times to stay on track? What kind of supervision/management facilitates your best work? Use any examples that apply to strengthen your response. In addition, make sure to think about the company to which you are applying and its culture. Management techniques are often dictated by company culture.

☞ "I enjoy working closely with my supervisor to accomplish organizational goals. For me, sitting down with management when a project is assigned and setting a schedule for checking in on my progress over the life of the project allows me to do my best work. My previous supervisor was great to work with for that reason. In addition, she was available for questions as they arose and did a nice job of helping me come to my own answers, increasing my skills and respect for good supervision."

Your answer: _____

_____

_____

_____

_____

_____

_____

_____

_____

71
DECISION MAKING

How do you make decisions?

Think about your decision-making process. A sample process is given here:

1. Define and clarify the issue.
2. Does it warrant action? If so, how?
3. Is the matter urgent, important, or both?
4. Gather all the facts.
5. Think about or brainstorm possible options and solutions.
6. Consider and compare the pros and cons of each option.
7. Consult with others, if possible.
8. Select the best option.
9. Explain your decision to those affected.
10. Follow up.

☞ "Decision making has been an important part of every job I've held in the past ten years. Early on, I realized that, without a specific process, I could make decisions too quickly, without having all of the necessary information. As a result, I am careful to define the problem or concern and gather as much information as possible before any decision is made. I then identify options—usually with some input from others who will be affected by the decision—consider the pros and cons of each option, and then decide. Although some minor decisions will require less effort, I still run through this process. Once the decision is made, I try to communicate it to everyone involved so we are able to move forward as a team."

Your answer: _____

_____

_____

_____

_____

_____

_____

_____

_____

_____

PROBLEM SOLVING

How do you solve problems?

Problem solving is a critical work skill in almost any job these days, so we recommend that you have a specific process in mind, such as the one written below. Remember, part of the point in problem solving is to solve the problem. The other part is to make sure that the problem doesn't occur again.

1. Identify the specific problem.
2. Review likely causes.
3. Break the problem down into manageable parts or components.
4. Gather the information you will need to identify problem-solving options.
5. Get input from others.
6. Choose a solution.
7. Make a plan to implement the solution.
8. Seek feedback about the success of the problem-solving process.

Use an example of a problem you have solved successfully in the past to answer this question. The following example uses the problem-solving process above without specifically enumerating the steps.

☞ "Solving problems successfully became increasing important as my company grew significantly over the last couple of years I worked for them. I remember one specific problem that occurred about a year ago. We were experiencing high levels of production waste in our manufacturing process and found that we would either have to reduce the amount of waste or raise our prices for finished products. We decided that our employees were not motivated to reduce waste, so we implemented a reward/punishment process on the work floor. Individual employees who reduced a week's waste at each station in which they worked got a gift certificate for fast food. Individuals whose waste increased were docked one hour of vacation time.

"The program was totally unsuccessful. When we sat down a second time to address this problem, we again identified the same problem, but this time we decided to meet with employees doing the work to see what they thought was happening. Imagine how surprised we were to find that our diverse work force, with many different native languages, had failed to understand what product they were producing, so they didn't understand the importance of getting the manufacturing process exactly right! We developed some training to make sure all of our employees understood our products, their uses, and the critical nature of exact specifications. Then we decided to reward teams and spend more time with those who were less successful instead of reducing their vacation time. Waste decreased by 50 percent in less than two weeks."

Your answer: _____

_____

_____

_____

_____

73
PROBLEM SOLVING

What do you do when you have trouble solving a problem?

Problem solving—the ability to think calmly and critically, generate options, and use good judgment— is one of the skills employers look for in all new employees. While we used to think that we could just go to work and "do our jobs" without much thought, most employees are now expected to solve problems. Think about how you go about solving problems and answer this question by talking about that process or by using an example from your work experience.

☞ "When I am faced with a difficult problem, I begin the solution by defining the problem. If I get the problem statement wrong, the chances of solving the problem are poor. If the problem is complex, I break it down into its individual pieces and gather both the people affected by the problem and the information needed to generate options. The best problem solving often requires a team effort. Once a solution is chosen, a plan can be developed. Then the causes of the problem can be reviewed and feedback on the solution obtained so that it doesn't occur again."

☞ "This question brings to mind a problem I was involved in solving recently. While working for a nonprofit organization that provides assistance to military families, our team was unable to meet our quarterly service goals. These goals are usually very easy to meet, so we were caught off guard. We scheduled a meeting to look at our service population and realized that our local Army post had deployed to Iraq more soldiers than we expected. What we discovered was that many of the families had returned home during their sponsor's deployment and therefore were not applying for continuing services. As a result, we realized that we needed to spend more time with our military counterparts so we could be realistic about our goals during future deployments."

Your answer: _____

_____

_____

_____

_____

_____

PROBLEM SOLVING

In this fast-paced environment we need someone who can think on his or her feet. What makes you this person?

Of all the questions you will encounter during an interview, this one requires the quickest answer. You must demonstrate your ability to "think on your feet" by not hesitating. The answer to this question is really focused on your ability to make decisions quickly, based on your knowledge and experience. To answer this question effectively, you will want to give concrete examples.

☞ "I was in a recent marketing strategy meeting where ideas were flying around faster than a flock of hummingbirds. It was very exciting to pick up on my colleagues' ideas and quickly develop marketing strategies that would effectively implement those ideas. One of the problems we had been struggling with was how to further penetrate existing accounts. My recommendation was to develop a "try and buy" program that allowed customers to test equipment before they purchased. My program was implemented, and the result was a $4 to $8 million increase in annual revenue."

Your answer: _____

_____

_____

_____

_____

_____

_____

_____

_____

_____

_____

_____

PROBLEM SOLVING

How do you deal with ambiguity (uncertainty or vagueness)?

Miscommunication at work is a common problem, and we are often more ambiguous in our communication than we intend to be. After all, you know what you mean; why shouldn't the person you are speaking with understand as well? To answer this question, think of a time when you thought you understood an assignment, single task, or offer to help and found that reality from someone else's point of view was quite different from your own.

☞ "I believe the best way to deal with ambiguity is to ask a lot of questions. The example that comes to mind for me occurred a few years ago. I had attended a meeting with a volunteer group planning a large community event. Each of us got an assignment to complete before the next meeting. Unfortunately, two of us completed the same assignment, having misunderstood what we had been asked to do. While we were able to work together to rectify the mistake after it was discovered, it took much longer to reach our goal. Since that time, I ask a number of questions about assignments and often send a note to the person with whom I am working, just to make sure I have been clear in my communication."

Your answer: _____

_____

_____

_____

_____

_____

_____

_____

_____

_____

_____

76
SUPERVISION

How do you evaluate the work of others?

This is a very broad question. Evaluating the work of others can include any experience, from generating formal feedback on work performance as part of an annual or semi-annual review to informal observations of employee work activities. What is important is that you include as many methods for gathering information as possible and that you briefly describe the importance of communicating the information with the employee in a timely manner. Remember, in order for employee evaluations to be effective, they must include behavioral information that can help the employee know what and how to change.

☞ "When I first began evaluating employees, I saw evaluation as a one-time event—something I did once a year. Now that I have more experience, I realize that employee evaluation is a constant part of employee supervision. I also know that evaluation is helpful to employees in improving their performance, just as it can be helpful to me in improving my performance. As a supervisor, I often check with other departments about the services my department provides to them. As a result, I get a lot of feedback about how my employees are doing. I take time to observe my department at work, looking for opportunities to compliment and reward individuals. I take notes—knowing I can't remember specific incidents without them—review random samples of employee work, pay attention to my conversations with employees about their impressions, and use the employee reward/concern forms my employer provides. In addition, in the annual review, the employee and I set performance goals for the following year, along with a schedule to review progress toward those goals so I am able to provide coaching. I stay in touch with the employee throughout the year to get each person's opinion about his or her own progress as well."

Your answer: _____

_____

_____

_____

_____

_____

_____

_____

77
SUPERVISION

How do you handle an angry employee?

If you have experience with this problem, you probably have both an example and a strategy for addressing it. If you haven't had such an experience, you can think of situations that included someone who was angry. In general, when someone is angry, you will want to remain calm and encourage the angry person to calm down as well. Remove the person to a private space as quickly as possible. Some people need to talk about their anger or the situation involved; others need time to process the event internally, so they will need time to think. The use of good listening skills, as well as appropriate statements of empathy, will help the employee through the process faster.

You can start by asking the angry person what you can do to help, and then set a time to meet and discuss the problem. Whether the person needs time alone or time to vent, problem solving cannot occur until afterward. When you meet to discuss whatever it was that created the anger, you will handle that meeting just as you would any employee performance conversation. Just in case, be prepared for a follow-up question about what you would do next.

☞ "I have some experience handling angry employees as a supervisor. Usually, the employee has been upset because a project he wanted was assigned to someone else or a performance review was less positive than the employee expected. I usually find it best to be specific and use neutral language when working with the employee individually. If the employee becomes angry, I schedule a follow-up appointment to continue the discussion later."

☞ "When an employee becomes angry at work, I try to get her to a private space as quickly as possible. That protects the employee and keeps others from taking sides in a dispute. Once we are alone, I will give the employee time to calm down. Walking to the private space usually helps with that. Sometimes a drink of water or a trip to the bathroom can provide additional time for the individual to calm down. After she is calm, a discussion of the issue that set off the anger and its solution can be discussed."

Your answer: _____

_____

_____

_____

_____

_____

_____

_____

_____

_____

SUPERVISION

What are some of the things your supervisor did that you disliked?

Your answer to this question will tell your interviewer a lot about how you like to be managed. You will be at a bit of a disadvantage, however, since you are either interviewing with your potential supervisor or with someone who possibly knows the management style of that person. If your answer reveals that you need "hands-on management" and the new supervisor uses a laissez-faire management style (or vice versa), then you might disqualify yourself from the job. Use anything you have noticed since you entered the interviewer's office (or waiting room) to judge what type of manager the person will be. Those clues will help to structure your answer. Oftentimes you won't have a clue, and in those cases, make your answer short, sweet, and to the point. Avoid too much negativity in your answer to this truly negative question. Instead, try to focus on how you adjusted to your supervisor's style and what you learned.

☞ "I have been fortunate to have some wonderful supervisors in my career. They appreciated my ability to take a project and run with it without requiring constant micromanagement. One of my supervisors, however, needed regular updates to feel in control. I didn't particularly like his management style, but I understood that I needed to honor it. I asked for a private meeting to communicate my own work preferences, and we came to a mutual understanding about what he needed so he could trust that I was on top of the project. I reported to him more often than I was accustomed to, and in the meantime he left me alone to do my job."

Your answer: _____

_____

_____

_____

_____

_____

_____

_____

_____

_____

_____

SUPERVISION

What experiences have you had that prepare you to supervise people who are older and more experienced than you?

If you have successful experience supervising people older than you, now is the time to share it, with specific examples. If you do not have that experience, think about any experiences you have with people older than you—volunteer, paid experience, or maybe just some time working with a neighbor. What the employer wants to know first is that you can work with people older than you, and secondly, that you can effectively supervise them.

☞ "I have two years of experience supervising others and feel that I could be very successful regardless of their ages. While I haven't supervised people older than I am, I have worked successfully with people older than I am on several projects. As a volunteer for the Boy Scouts of America, I worked on a Jamboree that was attended by more than 700 Scouts. I was responsible for coordinating space for tents with four other men, all older than I was by several years. We worked very well together and were able to arrange the land space without a single mix-up. I found working with an older person to be a great experience."

Your answer: _____

_____

_____

_____

_____

_____

_____

_____

_____

_____

_____

_____

LEADERSHIP

How would a subordinate describe your leadership style?

There are several very good theories about leadership style and performance. To answer this question, remember that you are being asked about how a subordinate would describe your style, not how you would describe it. Three basic forms of leadership that most buy into include authoritarian (autocratic, in-charge), participative (democratic, shared information gathering and/or decision making), and delegative (decision making is left to an employee). Each form has its advantages for both the leader and the followers, depending on the skill and experience of the employee and the difficulty and impact of the task to be completed. Most leaders use some of all three styles, with one style more dominant than the others. Again, you are describing a response you would expect to have a subordinate give in answer to this question.

☞ "I think most of my subordinates would say that I am a participative leader. I appreciate the opportunity to get their input on decisions whenever possible and like them to provide feedback on an informal basis whenever they can. Many decisions I will make on my own, after hearing their comments; some decisions can be team decisions. Under some circumstances, say, with a new employee, I am much more authoritarian until that person gets some experience in our work group. I think I am a delegative leader with employees who need new experiences in order to 'grow' their skills."

Your answer: _____

_____

_____

_____

_____

_____

_____

_____

_____

_____

_____

_____

LEADERSHIP

Describe a leader you admire.

There is a difference between a "manager" and a "leader." A manager **manages** the details of a project and ensures that things get done. A leader can be a manager, but generally a leader is seen as the person who provides the direction for an organization and then guides it along the path toward a goal. Ross Perot once said, "Inventories are managed. People must be led."

☞ "I admire the CEO of my current company more than any person I've worked for in the past. He is well informed, sets clear objectives, and inspires us to excel. He is truly charismatic, so I always leave our meetings energized and ready to give my best to achieve the goals he's set for the company."

Your answer: _____

_____

_____

_____

_____

_____

_____

_____

_____

_____

_____

_____

82
LEADERSHIP

How will you get along with a supervisor who is younger than you?

Obviously, the answer to this question is, "I will work well with a supervisor who is younger than I am." That is not, however, enough of an answer. In order for the interviewer to believe you, you need to provide an example of your ability to work with, or at least get along with, younger people.

☞ "I think I will get along well with a younger supervisor. In a couple of my current volunteer activities, I have worked closely with people much younger than I am. On the Denver Clean Environment Campaign, I worked with a group of ten people for three months to develop a plan for work assignments on Earth Day. We expected about 250 people to participate and were charged with identifying clean-up sites, assigning volunteer teams, and coordinating everyone's efforts on the day. Most of my group were people younger than I am and they had great ideas, a lot of energy to make things happen, and were fun to work with. The group leader was very young and pulled off our assignments without a hitch!"

Your answer: _____

_____

_____

_____

_____

_____

_____

_____

_____

_____

UNDER-/OVER-QUALIFIED

How do you think your lack of experience/degree will affect your ability to perform this job?

To answer this question, identify any areas of your background where you could be seen as "lacking experience." Focus on that area(s). Are you changing careers, jobs, or industries? Do you have education or training directly related to the job you are seeking? What are you doing to compensate for that missing experience at this time? Have you ever made a similar change in the past? How did you compensate at that time? How will you compensate once you start the job?

☞ "Although my experience is not in shipping and receiving, I have a lot of experience in manufacturing, and I am familiar with the contribution that a shipping and receiving department makes to product success and customer satisfaction. I have excellent attention-to-detail skills, am able to meet deadlines, and understand just-in-time materials-management policies from my experience in production."

☞ "Although I do not have a college degree, I do have a great deal of experience that would apply to this position. I have worked for two employers as a marketing assistant, moving up from an administrative assistant position. I am highly organized, work well with a wide variety of people, and find that I can add solid, creative ideas to my employer's marketing development process. In addition, I am currently enrolled in a marketing class at Pike's Peak Community College and hope to achieve an associate's degree over the next four years."

Your answer: _____

_____

_____

_____

_____

_____

_____

_____

_____

84
UNDER-/OVER-QUALIFIED

This job carries with it much more responsibility than you've had before. What makes you ready?

This question is really about being perceived as under-qualified for the position. It will be your job to convince the interviewer that you really are qualified. It could be that the interviewer doesn't see all of the qualifications on your résumé, so you will need to point them out. Perhaps your work experience didn't provide you with the skills needed, but you have non-work-related experience or formal education that does, so you will want to enumerate how each qualifies you for this new position. To do this effectively, however, you need to research the position as much as possible before the interview. Look for the key qualifications required in the job description and be prepared to address them. Use 3" x 5" cards and write each qualification on the top of a card, followed by your skills, education, or experience that relates. Focus on the positive and not why you aren't qualified.

☞ "I am ready for this level of responsibility. Even though my last job didn't require me to supervise direct reports, I have managed 20 volunteers at the American Red Cross on bi-monthly blood drives for the past five years. It was my responsibility to recruit, screen, and train them for their jobs, and then I scheduled, publicized, and coordinated each event, which often required working 14 hours a day and juggling resources and personnel to ensure that everything ran smoothly."

☞ "I have been preparing for this level of responsibility for more than four years. I've been attending the University of Phoenix at nights and will graduate next month with a Bachelor of Science in Business Administration. In my course work, I studied human resource management, business law, decision making, ethics, organizational development, and other subjects that directly relate to your job description. One of the things I like best about my studies is that our groups use the real work experiences of each team member to develop case studies and presentations for all of our classes. This has allowed me to gain insight into other companies besides my own and to work on real business problems that will transfer immediately to my new job."

Your answer: _____

_____

_____

_____

_____

_____

_____

_____

UNDER-/OVER-QUALIFIED

You appear to be overqualified for this job. What would cause you to take such a position at this time in your career?

There are several ways to answer this question. If you know that the company is young and/or growing, you can answer by focusing on how your skills will allow you to take off running from the first day in the position and then grow the job as the company grows. If you don't know enough about the position to make that assumption, then you will want to explain why circumstances in your life or changes in your career goals have made this new position ideal for you. Whatever you do, don't downplay your past experience or make excuses for your level of expertise.

For a rapidly growing company: "When I read about this job, I knew I could meet 100 percent of the requirements without a problem. Then I got to thinking about your new expansion initiative and how I could grow this position to directly benefit your new products. Instead of simply filling orders, I could develop a tickler system to follow up every 30 days. It would definitely increase customer satisfaction with your new products and at the same time provide me with an extra challenge."

For a change in your personal goals: "I had an opportunity for an information interview with Joe Morin and a tour of your print shop earlier this year. Joe seemed like an excellent manager, and the shop was well run and state-of-the-art. It made me realize how much I missed the smell of ink! When I saw your advertisement for a Customer Service Representative, I knew it was exactly what I wanted to do again. As you have probably noticed in my résumé, I was a CSR in the District Print Shop at Boulder Valley School District ten years ago. Since then, I gained diverse experience in all facets of design, layout, print production, offset printing, color separations, and trapping. Even though I enjoyed that work, at this point in my life I don't want that kind of pressure and frequent overtime again. I enjoy working with people, so the up-front customer service function of your position is especially appealing to me, and I would be happy to use my other skills to fill in occasionally when your work load requires it."

Your answer: _____

_____

_____

_____

_____

_____

STRENGTHS

What can you tell me that I do not already know about you that would make me hire you?

This is a strength question in disguise. You will need to think about what is on your résumé and what you have already told the interviewer. Then, think of a personal characteristic that you can add to the interviewer's knowledge of you. If you can relate the answer to a job qualification, so much the better.

☞ "I think you are learning that I have exactly the skills you need in this job. What you don't know is that I truly enjoy performing production work. As a result, I am pleasant to be around, enjoy producing a team product, and look forward to being highly productive on your assembly line."

Your answer: _____

_____

_____

_____

_____

_____

_____

_____

_____

_____

_____

_____

_____

87
STRENGTHS

What are your greatest strengths?

Don't provide a long list of adjectives here—hard working, intelligent, dedicated, honest, and so forth. Simple adjectives don't provide proof of your claims. You must give examples. Your interviewer is looking for a way to qualify (or disqualify) you from consideration, so you want to answer this question with strengths that directly relate to the position for which you are applying. For instance, if one of your greatest strengths is being compassionate, but you are seeking an aggressive sales position, then you could disqualify yourself if you focus on your compassion. On the other hand, if you are a nurse, then your compassion and empathy would be great strengths to emphasize. You can also include technical abilities or personality strengths that prove you will fit with the culture of the company and/or the team. Keep your list short, though. Choose three—or at the most five—of your strongest qualifications, and no more. If you don't provide enough concrete examples to prove your claims, be prepared to answer a follow-up question about the practical applications of your strengths.

☞ "One of my greatest strengths is my ability to build sales territories by using innovative marketing techniques. For instance, I developed a staff workshop for the surgical practices in my territory that increased sales of our new operating room instrument by 15 percent over the last six months. I am also very self-directed and have a strong work ethic that drove me to work 60 hours or more a week when I first broke into this market. I managed to capture 15 new accounts from a competitor and establish 95 new customers who generated $350,000 in new revenue in the first year. In the process, I developed a network of 200 possible accounts that I continue to work, although I am now more reasonable about the number of hours per week that I spend on my job."

Your answer: _____

_____

_____

_____

_____

_____

_____

_____

_____

_____

_____

STRENGTHS

What contribution do you anticipate being able to make to this position?

What contributions have you made to other positions you have held that are similar to the one for which you are applying? Contributions need to be specific and quantifiable, such as improved employee retention, increased work product produced, an improved way of accomplishing the work, development of a new product or service, and the list continues. If possible, an amount of time or money saved should be included in your answer. Be sure to review the job description and choose a contribution that will apply to the new job.

☞ "In a previous position, I was responsible for developing software with a team of engineers. We successfully brought four projects to completion in less than a year, breaking the record for my company in production. This job has similar responsibilities and I look forward to the opportunity to repeat that experience."

☞ "As office manager in my last position, I was able to increase work output enough to be able to decrease staff by one position. I was particularly proud of that experience because I had worked very hard to help my staff work well together and be able to cross-train. When one of our employees resigned to move across the state, we were able to absorb her work with our existing staff and morale remained high. Likewise, I hope I have the opportunity to improve productivity if I am offered this job."

Your answer: _____

_____

_____

_____

_____

_____

_____

_____

_____

STRENGTHS

What do your subordinates, coworkers, supervisors, and friends think are your strengths?

This is one of the most frequently asked questions in interviews. Be careful to craft your answer before the interview, because the interviewer will be listening for how you organize your thoughts, as well as what you say. Think about the job for which you are applying. Given the duties, what top three skills will be most critical to your performance on that job? Base your answer to this question around those strengths. Remember to couch your answer as a response to the way the question is being asked. Usually, the question will ask for one of these groups, not all. For example, "What do your coworkers think are your strengths?"

☞ "My coworkers would think my greatest strengths are in my ability to establish rapport and maintain a strong communication process over a long period of time. I enjoy working with a wide variety of people and that shows in my contacts with others. I generally communicate clearly with others and often follow a verbal communication with something in writing to confirm that everyone understands."

☞ "My supervisor would probably think about my strengths in software development and quality control. I pay close attention to detail, enjoy identifying glitches in software, and have exceptional problem-solving skills."

Your answer: _____

_____

_____

_____

_____

_____

_____

_____

_____

_____

WEAKNESSES

What is one of your biggest weaknesses on the job? What are some things that you find difficult to do? Why?

First, don't say that you don't have any weaknesses. Everyone has weaknesses, but you want to put a positive spin on yours. Often, weaknesses are really strengths that have been taken so far that they have become weaknesses. For instance, it's easy to take your attention to detail to the extreme of perfectionism. It's easy to have such high expectations for your own performance that you are unable to meet them regularly.

Regardless of your weakness, come up with a solution that overcomes it. Try to avoid personal characteristics and concentrate on more professional traits. Avoid pointing out weaknesses directly related to the job qualifications of the position for which you are applying.

☞ "I get so committed to a project that I sometimes lose sight of my personal need for rest. I often turn to my colleagues to remind me to take lunch breaks. If I don't take breaks, I become less effective and projects take longer."

☞ "I pride myself on being creative, but I have to admit that I sometimes miss the details. As a result, I always try to partner with someone on my team who is detail-oriented, and they tend to make up for this occasional weakness. If I find myself strictly on my own, I know I need a quiet place without interruptions to follow the details."

☞ "I sometimes base my decisions on feelings rather than on facts. Knowing that, I force myself to sit down and write a brief list of pros and cons before I follow through with decision making."

☞ "I have discovered that I can get lost in the details of a project and lose sight of the end result. My ability to manage details can easily become perfectionism if I'm not careful. To avoid this weakness, I check in with myself at the end of every day and evaluate my progress toward the project goal. I find that it keeps me on track so I meet my deadlines."

Your answer: _____

_____

_____

_____

_____

_____

WEAKNESSES

What might your current boss want to change about your work habits?

This is a tricky question. While we all have work habits that could benefit from change, you don't want to provide an answer to this question that could keep you from getting hired. Think of a work habit you have that can be turned into something you are working to change. Then address your awareness of your own behaviors at work and your willingness and ability to impact those habits.

☞ "I find that I become very focused at work, sometimes to the exclusion of the rest of my life. Eventually, I run out of energy and can't maintain that pace. Over the last year, my supervisor worked with me to set realistic goals and develop a more reasonable pace at work. The result was a much better balance of work and leisure activities."

☞ "I like meetings that start and end on time. When I am faced with several meetings in a row that start late and therefore end late, I find myself falling behind in my own goals for the day. What I have learned is that always starting and ending on time is not a realistic goal for every meeting, so now I plan for some meetings to run over time. While I still get frustrated, I no longer fall behind on my daily goals because of something that is out of my control."

Your answer: _____

_____

_____

_____

_____

_____

_____

_____

_____

WEAKNESSES

After six months on the job, what will be the most annoying thing about you?

Be careful here! You want to respond to this question without giving an example of something that could keep you from getting what you want—the job. Pick a habit or personal trait that, first, you can talk about; second, could irritate another without creating havoc; and third, won't interfere with your ability to perform your work.

☞ "Probably my desk. Although I am highly organized and my work is always done on time, my desk is regularly piled with stacks of work. As a result, my coworkers may assume that I am unorganized, unable to find things, or just plain messy. Actually, I straighten my desk a couple times a week, but the mess comes back. I can always find what I need, however, and I get my work done."

Your answer: _____

_____

_____

_____

_____

_____

_____

_____

_____

_____

SUCCESSES

How do you define success?

Webster's defines success as "the degree to which a task has a favorable outcome or attains a desirable end." Success is relative, however, and depends a great deal on what you find "desirable." Success can be measured by tasks—how well you write a letter or close a sale—or how well you have attained (or are on the road to attaining) your life goals—how much money you make, the size/value of your boat, or how well your kids do in school. In this answer, however, you will not want to focus on personal definitions of success. Again, your answer must relate to the job for which you are applying, or at least to work in general.

☞ "I define success as reaching my goals. It can be my goal to finish a project on time and on, or under, budget. Or it can be my goal to improve relationships with teammates so we work together more effectively. Anything I accomplish at work that helps me bring the company closer to its mission/vision statement is truly successful."

Your answer: _____

_____

_____

_____

_____

_____

_____

_____

_____

_____

_____

_____

SUCCESSES

What factors contribute the most to your success on your current job?

The interviewer asking this question could be seeking information about a number of your work behaviors and needs. For example, do you see your coworkers as contributing to your success? What kind of a work environment would be most conducive to your work success? What about your employer do you value most? Consider all these factors when developing your answer.

☞ "My current job gives me the opportunity to be both an individual contributor and a member of a closely knit team. As an individual contributor, I am challenged to do my best work. As a team member, I gather the enthusiasm from the entire group and see the results of my work in our products. As a result, I am successful in my work and feel a strong sense of accomplishment."

Your answer: _____

_____

_____

_____

_____

_____

_____

_____

_____

_____

_____

SUCCESSES

How do you explain your job successes?

Job success is related to many things, some of which are out of your control. Let's begin by looking at a definition of job success. You have the skills to perform the job, or you would not have this interview. Your success during the interview depends on your ability to explain your communication and personal skills, as well as your understanding of the importance of meeting employer expectations and getting along well with others.

☞ "I think job success depends on a number of factors, including having the necessary skills to perform the job. That's one of the reasons I would like the job you are offering—it capitalizes on skills I have worked hard to develop. In addition, communication with my supervisor, coworkers, and customers has been critical. I think that a willingness to learn new skills and my ability to meet supervisor expectations have played an important role in all my job successes. My previous supervisor will tell you that one of my strongest attributes is following through on my commitments."

Your answer: _____

_____

_____

_____

_____

_____

_____

_____

_____

_____

_____

FAILURES

Define the word "failure."

The Worldreference.com Dictionary defines failure as an unexpected omission, an act that fails, an event that does not accomplish its intended purpose, a person with a record of failing, or a lack of success.

☞ "Failure, to me, means not reaching an identified goal. That goal may be self-imposed or set by my supervisor or work group. Regardless of who sets the goal, I know that if I don't reach it, I have failed. Keeping my supervisor informed as to the progress or lack of progress on the goal is important. I like to make sure there are no surprises as the deadline approaches. I also know that it's important for me to learn from my failures, and I have."

Your answer: _____

_____

_____

_____

_____

_____

_____

_____

_____

_____

_____

97
FAILURES

What is the biggest work-related mistake you've made? What lessons did you learn?

"Work-related" is the key to answering this question correctly. Choose a mistake from your work life, not your personal life. The second part of this question is really the most important: you can make almost any mistake, as long as you learn from it. Being human, we all make mistakes, but you will want to pick one that is not too drastic so that you don't disqualify yourself from the job immediately. For instance, you would not want to admit to stealing from a past employer or to having used coercion from a position of power to get an employee to do something you wanted done.

☞ "I wish I were perfect and never made mistakes, but life just isn't like that. One of my biggest work-related mistakes was not clearing up a misconception about my computer skills. I hadn't been on my last job very long, but I had already developed a reputation as an expert with Microsoft Office and other business software. Well, my boss asked me to create something in Adobe Photoshop, and I told him I could do it. I didn't have any experience with the software, but everyone assumed that I did. Instead of telling him that I would need help, I tried to do the job myself. The finished project didn't turn out very well. I learned that it's okay not to know everything, and that it's better to ask for help at the very beginning of a project. I also learned that the end result is more important than my ego."

Your answer: _____

_____

_____

_____

_____

_____

_____

_____

_____

_____

ACCOMPLISHMENTS

What achievements have eluded you?

You want to answer this question truthfully, with a positive spin. Once you discuss an achievement that has eluded you, talk about what you've learned from that experience. Also, don't forget that you are still achieving, so you might realize the achievement at a later time. Another way to answer this question is to talk about the goals you set when you originally started to work. Then you can speak to any achievements you didn't reach as your goals changed.

☞ "When I got out of college, I wanted to be a high school teacher. Unfortunately, no positions were available then, due to a glut of teachers. I was terribly disappointed because I really felt I had a gift to teach. After a couple of months working in a local department store, a job became available that allowed me to teach life skills to adults who had suffered head injuries and needed to learn self-care all over again. I took the job and loved the work for several years. I guess my goal to teach was still there, but my need to do that within a school setting had changed. Whenever I have suffered a setback, I use this example to help me see that no need is satisfied by only one solution."

Your answer: _____

_____

_____

_____

_____

_____

_____

_____

_____

_____

_____

CHARACTERISTICS/PERSONALITY

Describe your personality.

The best way to come up with an answer to this question is to ask your friends or coworkers how they would respond to this question for you. Make sure to ask them to focus on work characteristics and skills in their answers. Then, craft your answer using their responses.

☞ "I'm an outgoing person. I enjoy working with others and developing opportunities to get to know new people as well. My energy level is high and I like to be busy. Friends tell me that there is 'never a dull moment' in my life, and I think they're right. I always have something going on. These characteristics show up on the job when I become a team player and take on challenges. In my last position, I worked on a short-term project with a team whose members were based all over the United States. My communication skills, 'can-do' positive attitude, and willingness to put in extra time to meet the deadline were instrumental in bringing the project in on time."

Your answer: _____

_____

_____

_____

_____

_____

_____

_____

_____

_____

CHARACTERISTICS/PERSONALITY

What personal quality makes you the perfect hire for this position?

Here's your chance to talk about your personality, finally! Think back to your past performance evaluations, letters of recommendation, and conversations where you have chatted about your personal strengths. What positive traits do people tend to see in you? Which ones make you feel the most proud? Choose one of those personal qualities and relate it to the workplace.

☞ "I am the perfect hire for this position because I'm driven by a need to learn new things. For instance, just last year, I signed up for three Steven Covey seminars. I learned a lot about goal setting and motivating workers to achieve company goals. Since you are in an industry that is constantly changing, this ability to quickly assimilate new ideas and ways of doing things makes me ideally suited for this position. I will be able to hit the ground running from the first day on the job and keep up with the ever-shifting responsibilities of a project manager in the telecommunications industry."

Your answer: _____

_____

_____

_____

_____

_____

_____

_____

_____

_____

_____

_____

CHARACTERISTICS/PERSONALITY

What are your pet peeves?

This is another example of a question that can be tough to answer. You need to be honest, while not including "peeves" that are likely to interfere with your ability or motivation to do the new job. You do need to be able to talk about how you deal with your irritation when faced with a pet peeve. Examples of pet peeves might include meetings that are disorganized or run late; having to work in close quarters with someone who has a strong body odor or bad breath; or depending on someone who is always late.

☞ "One of my pet peeves at work is wastefulness. I have worked for companies in the past that never checked to see who in town could provide us with office or production supplies in the fastest and most cost-effective manner. When I come across that situation now, I begin by asking my supervisor if I can do some research into suppliers in our area. I then collect the data and provide it in a short report with comparisons. I also recognize that the least expensive supplier may not be the best supplier for our company."

Your answer: _____

_____

_____

_____

_____

_____

_____

_____

_____

_____

_____

102
CHARACTERISTICS/PERSONALITY

Do you prefer working as a member of a team or would you rather work alone? Why?

The research you have performed on this company could give you some insight into your answer to this question. Does the job for which you have applied require teamwork or will most of your job duties be performed individually? Most jobs require a mix of team and individual contributor skills.

☞ "I actually prefer to work on a team, but I also perform well when I work alone. My research on your company indicated that you offer a team environment and that is one of the things that attracted me. While much of my work will be completed individually, everyone here appears to be attached to a department with a director who manages the teamwork."

Your answer: _____

_____

_____

_____

_____

_____

_____

_____

_____

_____

_____

_____

103
CHARACTERISTICS/PERSONALITY

Describe how you establish your credibility.

First, let's define "credibility." Credibility, in this context, can be defined as "authenticity, reliability, and believability"; in other words, trustworthiness. With that definition, think about all the ways you determine if another person is credible. Those are the characteristics you want to include in your answer. The following questions might help direct your thoughts:

- From whom do you seek advice? Why?
- Does the person speak truthfully, without exaggerating or shading the truth?
- Can you rely on this person to behave in a predictable manner?
- Is "what you see is what you get" the rule, or do you wonder about hidden agendas when interacting with this person?

- When you have received advice from this person in the past, has it been good advice? If you chose not to take his/her advice, how did the person react?
- Which of these characteristics that establish credibility are true of you?

☞ "Establishing credibility is an important part of any new job. Team members and the staff who depend on me for their work product must see me as credible and effective in my work. As a result, I begin a job by prioritizing learning my new work responsibilities and getting to know the people with whom I work. Part of getting to know others is giving them time to get to know me as well. I am careful to honor my commitments on the time schedule I agree to. I ask questions and expect others to question me if I am not clear in my communication with them. If any problems occur, I address them immediately by apologizing for my mistakes or misunderstandings without allowing problems to grow or damage relationships. I don't engage in gossip, I always try to tell the truth in a way that is respectful of my coworkers, and I listen to others to make sure I understand their expectations. As a result, once credibility is established, it's easy to maintain."

Your answer: _____

_____

_____

_____

_____

_____

_____

_____

_____

MOTIVATION

What motivates you to put forth your best effort?

What causes you to perform your best work? Don't be shy about the answer. Is it public acknowledgement or just the personal satisfaction of a job well done? Is it having others depend on you, meeting a deadline, knowing you will get paid a certain amount of money, having a quiet space, knowing the goal of the work but not being told how to achieve it? Try to frame your answer in the context of the job for which you are applying.

☞ "I work best in a cooperative, team environment. I like the stimulation of hearing many different ideas, coming to group consensus, planning how to move forward, and then taking on my part of a project. I look forward to team meetings to coordinate project components and appreciate having a deadline for completion."

☞ "I perform my best work when I have a specific goal in mind and can be creative in my methods to reach that goal. I like to work independently, consulting regularly with my supervisor to maintain lines of communication."

☞ "I am motivated by the sense of satisfaction I get when a job is completed and done right the first time."

☞ "I really liked those little certificates my supervisor gave me when I exceeded my quotas. It made me feel like I was making a difference at my last company. I suppose that recognition motivates me to sell more."

Be prepared for the interviewer to ask you for an example with any of these answers.

Your answer: _____

_____

_____

_____

_____

_____

_____

_____

MOTIVATION

What two or three things are most important to you in your job?

Interviewers who ask this question are usually looking for what you personally value about your work. Is it challenge, advancement opportunities, recognition, independence, creative expression, variety, travel, good relationships with coworkers and the boss, prestige, making a contribution, or helping others? Next, think about how your work values fit with the job for which you are applying and include that information in your answer.

☞ "For me, the most important aspect of any job is my ability to make a contribution to the organization I work for. I like to perform a variety of duties, and I know that seeing different clients will keep this job from becoming too routine."

☞ "I like to be challenged in my work, so problem solving for a customer who is experiencing difficulty is something I look forward to. My sense of satisfaction once the problems are solved is really important to me."

Your answer: _____

_____

_____

_____

_____

_____

_____

_____

_____

_____

_____

_____

106
MOTIVATION

What do you think determines a person's progress in a company?

An interviewer who asks this question is often looking for your sense of personal responsibility for making things happen. Think about the job you are interviewing for. What qualities will be important to your employer for you to be considered a great employee? Don't forget to do your research. A company's literature will usually provide your answer.

☞ "I think people progress in a company based on their ability to get things done and done well. Strong communication skills, a willingness to pitch in where I am needed, and a commitment to producing a high-quality product (or service) will result in positive progress for me."

Your answer: _____

_____

_____

_____

_____

_____

_____

_____

_____

_____

_____

_____

VALUES

For what would you like to be remembered?

This is a fairly straightforward question, and it should be answered in the same manner. There is no hidden meaning here. Your answer will tell the interviewer what you value the most. As with most interview questions, your answer should address values that have meaning in the workplace—hard work, integrity, leadership, the ability to work as a valued team member/leader, willingness to go the extra mile, and the list continues.

☞ "Although I hope it won't be too soon, someday I want the epitaph on my headstone to read: 'She worked hard and made a difference in her corner of the world.'"

Your answer: _____

_____

_____

_____

_____

_____

_____

_____

_____

_____

_____

_____

_____

108
ETHICS

How would your last employer describe your work ethic?

Every interviewer wants to hear that you have a strong work ethic, but you can't just say it. You have to **prove** it with an example. So, what proves that you have a strong work ethic? Your answer might include working long hours to meet a deadline or being productive by making good use of every minute you are on your employer's time clock. Be careful not to overdo it, however. If you tell your interviewer that you regularly work 10 or 12 hours a day, you might be perceived as being unable to use time efficiently or as having poor business judgment.

☞ "I was raised to believe that the world doesn't owe me a living. I've always tried to give my employers a fair day's work—and more—for my pay. My last employer would tell you that I was willing to work overtime to get a project out the door on time and that I worked efficiently and productively every day."

Your answer: _____

_____

_____

_____

_____

_____

_____

_____

_____

_____

_____

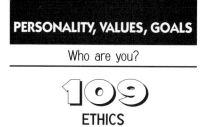

109

ETHICS

What have you ever kept or taken from your employer to which you felt entitled?

You don't want to be surprised by this question! The worst answer is probably "nothing." That's because it is common practice in our work environments to fax personal information when expedient, make an occasional copy or two of personal records, or use the telephone at work to make a personal call. In addition, think about the employer's pens, pencils, paperclips, and other small items that find themselves in your purse or pockets at the end of a long day. While none of this may constitute stealing, you are using office machines and supplies for purposes other than work.

☞ "I don't believe that I have ever taken anything from an employer that I intentionally meant to take. However, as I think about this question, I realize that I have, on occasion, used company machines, such as a copier, fax, or computer to complete personal business, and I suppose that could be construed as 'taking something from my employer' because I didn't specifically ask to use the machines in that way. In addition, I regularly complete some work from home and I know that the leftover pens, pencils, highlighters, or sticky notes don't always go back to the office."

Your answer: _____

_____

_____

_____

_____

_____

_____

_____

_____

_____

_____

_____

_____

110
ETHICS

What do you, as an employee, owe your boss and what does your boss owe you?

The phrase that comes to mind every time I see this question is "an honest day's pay for an honest day's work." While that might be the bare minimum of what the agreement between employer and employee is all about, both parties look for more than that in today's labor market. You must evaluate what you really expect from your employer and what you are willing to give in return.

☞ "I believe that accepting a job is akin to signing a contract, whether I sign a piece of paper or not. I agree to work hard, to work to the best of my ability, demonstrating honesty, integrity, and respect. In return, I expect my employer to be honest, display a high level of integrity, pay me according to our agreement, and respect me for my contributions."

Your answer: _____

_____

_____

_____

_____

_____

_____

_____

_____

_____

_____

_____

111

ETHICS

What tips can you bring to us from your previous company?

Watch your answer here! The interviewer is testing your integrity and, at the same time, trying to determine if you will be able to bring something of value from your previous employer—contacts, new clients, and expertise, among other things. What you don't want to do is to give away trade secrets, confidential company information, or anything else you know your previous employer would not want a competitor to know. You need to walk a very fine line between giving away too much and saying too little.

☞ "I have been working in new product development at XYZ Company for the past seven years. Confidentiality is extremely important in our business, so I'm not free to discuss products that are currently in the pipeline. However, I have gained considerable experience in the development process that will be extremely valuable to you, as will my contacts with raw material suppliers worldwide."

Your answer: _____

_____

_____

_____

_____

_____

_____

_____

_____

_____

_____

GOAL SETTING

Describe a major goal you have recently set for yourself.

If you are not in the habit of "conscious living" (regularly evaluating your values, setting goals, and making choices every day that align with your values and goals), then you need to start now. So many people let life simply happen and never consciously make choices about how to spend their time. Don't be one of those. Before your first interview, decide what makes you happy and what will make a difference in your circle of influence. Then set reasonable goals to help you align your life—your every moment—with your values. Thank heaven you are reading this book now, because you can make these changes before the interview where this question will be asked. Now that you have set some goals, you can choose one that relates to the job for which you are applying.

☞ "I believe in living consciously. I don't want to waste a minute of my life, because I can never get it back once it has passed. I regularly evaluate what I want, set goals, and make daily choices that help me achieve those goals. Recently, I decided that being a licensed counselor in my state wasn't enough. I needed to get a coaching certification to make me more valuable to college career centers like yours. I have already completed four of the eight classes I need and will complete the others within the next six weeks. This credential will enhance the credibility of your career center if I'm hired, and it gives me the training I need to perform at a much higher level."

Your answer: _____

_____

_____

_____

_____

_____

_____

_____

_____

_____

_____

_____

GOAL SETTING

Where would you see yourself in five years? (long-range goals)

The interviewer is interested in knowing whether your goals and the company goals are compatible. Look at the job description, to whom you would be reporting, and where the position lies within the organizational chart. Review your research on the company. If they are growing and anticipate continuing growth, your desire to grow long term in the company would be a compatible goal. Next, look at your job history. How has your work experience or education and training background affected your goals or motivation? What new skills do you want to gain? Now compose your answer to this question.

☞ "A lot can happen over five years and my long-term goals, to some extent, depend on my next job and what skill growth I need to perform that job well. I do know that you are a small business and expect to grow significantly over the next five years. That's one of the reasons I'm seeking work with your company—it provides me with an opportunity for growth into a supervisory position. I was a first-time supervisor in my last position and really enjoyed supervising others. While I was successful, I learned that I need additional experience in leadership. Improving those skills would be another of my long-term goals."

☞ "The position we are discussing today will take me in the direction I want to go over the next five years. It would allow me to make a significant contribution to a new product, and that's the reason I'm interested in working for you. I have been successful in product development in the past and look forward to fine tuning those skills with your company. In addition, this position would expose me to customers and I am interested in enhancing my customer service skills."

Your answer: _____

_____

_____

_____

_____

_____

_____

_____

114

GOAL SETTING

What career or business would you consider if you were starting over again?

Would you hire me if I told you that I wanted to be a full-time artist when I "grew up" when you were offering me a job as an accountant? Of course not. You would be concerned that I wouldn't be working where my passion lies. So, you need to answer this question within the position and/or industry where you are applying. It's perfectly fine to start out with a different career or business and then lead into why you chose to be an accountant, for instance.

☞ "When I graduated from high school, I wanted to be a veterinarian, but my family couldn't afford the many years of college it would take to get there. I started college on an athletic scholarship and took a part-time job with a local newspaper. After I graduated with a communications degree, I was so thankful that I hadn't pursued my original dream. I am really passionate about the research and writing that is part of my journalism career."

Your answer: _____

_____

_____

_____

_____

_____

_____

_____

_____

_____

_____

GOAL SETTING

What skills would you like to develop in this job?

This question is about what you can contribute as well as what skills you want to learn, so your answer should include information about both areas. What skills could you learn in the job for which you are applying? Also, think about your goals for new skill growth. The intersection of the two should help you compose your answer.

☞ "My experience in providing service to customers is extensive and successful. I enjoy those duties and feel I could be an asset to your company in that area. In addition, the position for which I am applying would allow me to direct the work of a group. While I have some experience in supervision, I look forward to managing a customer service group and applying some of my skills in a different direction. Problem solving on a group level, planning for continuous improvement, team development, and leadership are all skills I can develop and fine-tune on this job."

Your answer: _____

_____

_____

_____

_____

_____

_____

_____

_____

_____

116

GOAL SETTING

Why did you choose this career?

While many of us "fall into" careers rather than making conscious choices, stating that your career choice is based on an accident is probably not the best way to respond to this question. Even those of us who found our careers without specific choice usually can find a reason for moving into whatever career we are in. You might have had a job in high school or college that piqued your interest in a particular career and you therefore got the training you needed to work in that industry. You may have a parent who influenced your choice, a teacher or a class you took that pushed you in a new direction, or a friend's job that looked so interesting you decided to pursue it as a career yourself.

☞ "When I entered college, I didn't have much job experience, and I had always liked my history classes, so I decided to major in history. By the end of my freshman year, I realized that I enjoyed my English classes so much that I decided to take a journalism course. That course changed my major, my career goals, and my life. I can't imagine taking any job that didn't require writing as a primary skill because I really enjoy putting my thoughts down on paper."

Your answer: _____

_____

_____

_____

_____

_____

_____

_____

_____

_____

_____

117

GOAL SETTING

What do you hope to be doing two years from now? (short-term goals)

This can be a tough question because you have to guess where you might go within a company over a two-year period of time, and you have to be able to talk about how you might get there. First, research the company. Where is the company likely to be in two years? Will it grow, providing you with new opportunities, or does its history indicate that it will stay about the same size? How does this company fit with your short- and long-term career plans?

☞ "Two years from now, I hope to have a clear understanding of the products we produce and all aspects of the production process. Long-term, I am interested in managing a department, so I would hope to have begun supervising some work functions within the next two years."

☞ "I want to be the best at my job. Right now, I am good at providing exceptional customer service. But I will be able to take those skills to even higher levels of performance after two years of contributing to your customers. Long-term, I am interested in working with key accounts on multifaceted projects to make sure they get every possible benefit our product has to offer."

Your answer: _____

_____

_____

_____

_____

_____

_____

_____

_____

_____

_____

_____

118
GOAL SETTING

Have you ever taken a position that didn't fit into your long-term plan? How did it work out for you?

If your career has taken a straight path toward a specific job, you probably won't be asked this question, or at least you won't have to answer it with anything besides, "No, all of my positions have fit into my long-term plan." If, on the other hand, your job history is a little more "checkered" and you've had a variety of experiences, you will need to expect this question and develop an answer. A position that didn't fit into your long-term plans could be one that you took because it looked interesting at a time when you were job seeking, a position that followed a job loss and served to fill a gap while you looked for another job, or even a job you took to help out a friend. What is important is that you learned new information or enhanced your skills in some way.

☞ "Early in my career, when I found myself without a job due to a layoff, I took a position as a sales clerk for a small downtown bookstore. While the job didn't fit into my career path, it did teach me a different perspective on work, and I got a chance to learn about the wide range of skills required to manage a small business. While the owners did their own bookkeeping, we all knew how to tally the day's sales and make the deposit. We were trained in stocking, sales, and money collection. In addition, we had input into the ordering of new books based on our customer contacts. My customer service skills really improved, and I gained increased respect for really good teamwork."

Your answer: _____

_____

_____

_____

_____

_____

_____

_____

_____

_____

PROGRESS TOWARD GOALS

What accomplishments have you made so far in reaching your long-range goals?

You want your interviewer to come away from your answer with the impression that you know what you want in life and are working hard to get there. The question that usually precedes this one is "What are your long-range goals?" It will be helpful for you to relate your "accomplishments answer" to the answer you previously gave about your long-range goals.

☞ "One of my long-range goals is to acquire more leadership skills so I can become an even better manager. To accomplish this, I have started working on my MBA at ABC College in the evenings. I expect to graduate next year at about this time. In addition, I was selected for my current employer's mentoring program two years ago. I requested that my mentor be the senior vice president of my division. I truly admire her leadership abilities, and she has already taught me a great deal about being a good leader."

Your answer: _____

_____

_____

_____

_____

_____

_____

_____

_____

_____

_____

120

PROGRESS TOWARD GOALS

How do you feel about your career progress to date?

If ever there was a time to think positively about your career progress, this is it! Career progress is in the eye of the beholder, so you can talk about it from a positive perspective regardless of what you have done or where you have worked. If you have had several jobs in different industries or even different departments, you can speak to your diversity of experiences and varied skills. If you have focused in one or two areas, you can speak to your depth of knowledge. You can also talk about your job experiences in terms of your changing needs. Be sure to end your answer with a clear statement about how your career progress to date can benefit the interviewer's company.

☞ "I am happy with the progression of my career to this point. I have had a variety of experiences in nonprofit, for-profit, and government agency environments. I feel that I have significantly contributed to the skills and personal development of my clients and the well being of my employers. The range of skills I have been fortunate to gain is wide and fits well with the job for which I am applying."

Your answer: _____

_____

_____

_____

_____

_____

_____

_____

_____

_____

_____

121
PROGRESS TOWARD GOALS

What career path interests you within the company?

It is perfectly fine to expect promotions and see yourself in another job within the company in the future. At the same time, however, you don't want the interviewer to feel like you won't be happy for long in the job for which you are applying. Your answer should focus on the typical career path in your industry (staff accountant to manager to partner, for example). If you don't know what that career path should be, it is all right to ask, "What do you see as the typical career path in your company for someone in my position?" Then you answer the original question based on the information provided by the interviewer.

☞ "I see myself eventually moving up from a supervisor on the assembly line to a production manager or perhaps specializing in quality control management. I really enjoy our industry and gain a lot of satisfaction from seeing a well-made product at the end of the process."

☞ "After working as a teacher for a number of years, I have in-depth knowledge of how to reach students. I am excited to use that background as a foundation for making your school even better as an assistant principal. Eventually, I would like to become the principal of this school, so I can have even more impact. To accomplish that, I am planning to return to college for my administrator's certification and perhaps even a Ph.D."

Your answer: _____

_____

_____

_____

_____

_____

_____

_____

_____

_____

NON-WORK ACTIVITIES/OUTSIDE INTERESTS

What are your leisure-time activities?

Interviewers ask this question for a couple of reasons. They want to see if you have a balanced lifestyle. They want to make sure you are well-rounded. They want to see if you are a health risk—couch potato or extreme sports participant (visions of way too much sick leave!). Or, are you too busy and headed for burnout? Avoid controversial activities in your answer at all costs—religion, politics, extremist activities. As a general rule, you are safe to talk about community service or other people-oriented interests— Toastmasters, Boy or Girl Scouts, Big Brothers/Sisters, Lions Club, Rotary—you get the idea. You can pick up clues about the company's community orientation from trophies, plaques, and other items you might have noticed on your way into the interview. Sometimes an Internet search or the company's Web site will turn up articles or tidbits of information that you can use to develop your answer to this question. Of course, anything that relates to your job is even better to mention—active member in the local Chamber of Commerce, Better Business Bureau, or industry trade association.

☞ "I have several hobbies that I really enjoy in my spare time, including gardening and training my two dogs. I sit on the board of directors of both the Boy Scouts and the Young Entrepreneurs Association, which gives me an opportunity to influence our future generation of leaders."

Your answer: _____

_____

_____

_____

_____

_____

_____

_____

_____

_____

_____

_____

NON-WORK ACTIVITIES/OUTSIDE INTERESTS

What is the best book you've read in the last year? What did you like about it?

Answers to this question can be quite revealing about your personality, interests, hobbies, religion, work, education level, and any number of facts that you may or may not want a potential employer to know about you, so think carefully before you respond.

☞ "My library contains a mixture of books, but my favorites are books about …"

- Religion—too much information an employer shouldn't know.
- Literature—good quality books that say you have an education.
- Philosophy—same goes here.
- History—serious.
- Languages—great in today's global society.
- Science Fiction—most are okay and can even give you something to talk about in the interview, unless they are wayyyyy out there!
- Fantasy—okay, especially if they are classics like Tolkien, C.S. Lewis, Terry Brooks, and so on.

- Romance—may be too light for many interviewers, who won't take you seriously.
- Math and Science—good backup for those types of careers.
- Your Trade—same goes for these books.
- How-To—great for those who like to build things themselves or who find that quality helpful in their careers.
- Comics—you know, for investment purposes only!

☞ "I like the fact that reading _____ provides me with a way to relax after an intense day at work. Because I frequently read books related to our industry, I continue growing and getting better at what I do each day. I recently finished <u>Good to Great</u> and found it especially insightful into what makes a company truly great—staying true to the organization's original values, goals, mission, and core competencies regardless of what the crowd is doing. I find that very gutsy and inspiring."

Your answer: _____

_____

_____

BARRON'S

Behavioral questions seek information about your past experiences, which are indicators of future performance. If you saved your previous employer money, you will probably do the same for your new employer. If you improved customer service in the past, you can to do it again. Behavioral questions are always about the past.

Situational questions, on the other hand, are all about the future. What would you do if…? They require you to think creatively and to role play. You can basically make up your answer, but the answer will be much stronger if you include an example from your past experience.

You can recognize either of these types of questions quickly because they almost always start with: "Tell me about…," "Describe a situation where…," "Give me an example of…," or "What would you do if…?"

The interviewer will be specific when asking these questions, so you should be specific in your answer as well. Create a story that demonstrates your ability to perform the tasks in question. An example is always much better than a simple statement, and the interviewer is expecting to hear a story.

All good stories have a beginning, middle, and end, so tailor your response like a story you would tell your children at bedtime. The story must be well organized and succinct, or your listener will get lost. Telling the story in chronological order helps make it easier to follow and more interesting. Remember the simple STAR acronym when you structure your response:

S = Describe the **S**ituation or

T = **T**ask that was causing a problem. These two letters represent the background of the story.

A = What **A**ction did you take? What was your reaction to the situation? This part of the answer is always the longest.

R = What was the **R**esult of your action? How did it turn out? What did you learn that contributes to your work skills?

Practice your stories well in advance of your interview. Tape recording them often helps. When you play back the recording, listen to your tone of voice. Do you sound positive, enthusiastic, and upbeat? Is the story short, sweet, and to the point? Are there parts of your answer you can delete without affecting the story itself? If you were the interviewer, would you hire yourself?

INTERPERSONAL RELATIONSHIPS/TEAMS

Tell me about a work group you really enjoyed.

To answer this question, you want to talk about the work group and include information about how that group helped you to meet the requirements of your job. Add anything you learned about work from that experience.

☞ "My first job out of college was at the state prison as a rehabilitation counselor. What could have been an overwhelmingly negative environment was transformed into a positive experience by the work team. Two counselors, two secretaries, and a psychologist worked together to place inmates in job assignments and conduct pre-release planning. We met twice a week to discuss our active cases and get feedback on released clients from other rehabilitation offices across the state. Often we combined our meeting with lunch so we could have some time together away from the institution. I have, throughout my career, thought about the leader of that team and his skills in team development and team maintenance. I have worked to make many of those skills a part of my repertoire."

Your answer: _____

_____

_____

_____

_____

_____

_____

_____

_____

_____

INTERPERSONAL RELATIONSHIPS/TEAMS

Tell me about a business need you fulfilled within a group or a committee.

Think about a business need where you have been the key person responsible for fulfilling that need. You can use a volunteer activity like the one used in the example that follows, a work example, or a personal one. It is important that you explain the business need well, and how you contributed to the resulting success.

☞ "As a member of a local school board, I was assigned to a food service committee that included the superintendent, two parents, and our director of nutrition services. The purpose of the committee was to improve our lunch and breakfast program, increasing the availability of healthy foods as well as the cost-effectiveness of the program. We asked parents and students, K–12, to complete a survey with questions about food likes and dislikes, health needs, and nutrition. When the survey was returned, it was clear we needed to make some changes and the debate became very emotional. I took all the data, transferred it to a spreadsheet, and presented the information in a matter-of-fact manner. As a result, committee members were able to reduce their emotional responses and work effectively together, making a data-driven decision."

Your answer: _____

_____

_____

_____

_____

_____

_____

_____

_____

INTERPERSONAL RELATIONSHIPS/TEAMS

Tell me about a time when you persuaded others to take action.

You could have persuaded coworkers to take action, contributed to a boss's decision about a problem or planning need, or worked on a committee where you made a substantial contribution. Think of something you were able to accomplish by working with others in a leadership role.

☞ "I had worked in food service for a number of years when I was hired by a staffing agency as a sales representative to work with current clients and expand our client base. While I was willing to 'beat the pavement,' using the traditional methods for generating business, I also recommended that the company join a few professional and industry groups to generate more excitement and awareness about our company. Although the owner was skeptical about the idea, he finally agreed to allow me to join the local Chamber of Commerce. Business improved by 10 percent in less than four months. By the end of the year, we belonged to several groups and our staffing business had a new problem— the need for qualified workers!"

Your answer: _____

_____

_____

_____

_____

_____

_____

_____

_____

INTERPERSONAL RELATIONSHIPS/TEAMS

Let me describe the work group you would be joining if we hired you. How would you fit in? What would you see as your role as a team member/builder?

An example of a work group might include a newly formed team of previously individual contributors that could benefit from someone with a strength in communication. Another example would be a team that has been together for a long time and has to accept a new member. That team would need someone who is flexible enough to observe the existing team dynamics and fit in where needed.

☞ "From what you describe, it sounds like you could use a team builder. As a newly hired sales manager at XYZ Company, I found myself managing a team of people who hadn't worked together before. In addition, we needed to set up our standard operating procedures. To accomplish both the business needs and begin some team building, each team member and I took one section of the policy and procedures manual and developed a draft statement from researched information. Then we met as a team, reviewed the drafts, and completed the project. Next, we created documents to standardize our sales process and developed a staff meeting schedule to share best practices and discuss problems. My role as the team leader was to keep the process moving and make sure that everyone's opinion was heard. I would bring similar team-building skills to your work group."

Your answer: _____

_____

_____

_____

_____

_____

_____

_____

_____

_____

INTERPERSONAL RELATIONSHIPS/TEAMS

You have a history of not getting along with a coworker. Your boss has just asked the two of you to work together on a project. What do you do?

Remember that a situational question is seeking an answer to a hypothetical situation. You can make up an answer or use an example from real life. The interviewer's goal is to evaluate your problem-solving skills.

☞ "First, I would take the initiative to try to resolve the underlying problem that has been making it hard for the two of us to work together in the past. I would find a quiet, private place for the two of us to meet. Then I would let my coworker know that I am willing to put any problems of the past behind us, so we can succeed on this new project. If she wants to talk about the past, then I will listen and reflect her feelings back to her so she feels validated. Hopefully this will build a foundation of trust for the new project. If problems continue, I would request mediation from our supervisor."

Your answer: _____

_____

_____

_____

_____

_____

_____

_____

_____

_____

_____

_____

CUSTOMER SERVICE

Describe a time when your customer service skills and diplomacy have been put to the test.

Customer service skills have become a necessary skill set in almost any job in today's marketplace. This question is asking for a specific example, so think about your experience working with customers and identify an example of one of your most difficult customer service situations.

☞ "When working in a retail setting just before I graduated from college, I encountered a customer who had experienced a very negative customer service situation in our store. As a result, she was ready to take my head off at the first sign of a problem. She requested a specific product that we did not have in stock, and although I offered to order it and showed her several similar products, she was not interested. As we talked, she became increasingly upset. I made sure to let her talk as much as she wanted, listened carefully to her complaints, and eventually ordered the product, having it shipped overnight. At my request, the store agreed to assume the cost of shipping and we were able to get the product delivered to her home the next day. My boss complimented my listening skills and willingness to understand the customer's complaint as the reason this situation ended well for the store."

Your answer: _____

_____

_____

_____

_____

_____

_____

_____

_____

_____

CUSTOMER SERVICE

You work in the billing department of a large firm. A customer's order was delayed for unknown reasons, and when she called to complain, she was cut off twice. Now she is calling again. How will you handle her phone call?

Before answering this question, think about the company's philosophy of customer service discovered during your research process. Try to integrate that philosophy into your answer. Always address providing a solution to preventing the problem in the future, so your interviewer knows that you are proactive.

☞ "First, I would apologize for the problem and go over her concerns with her, making sure I have all of the information I need. The most important goal is to get the product to the customer, so I would make sure her order was refilled and sent out the same day, with upgraded shipping. A quick call back to the customer to let her know when to expect her package would help to manage her expectations. I would then make sure to research the root cause of the delay to avoid a reoccurrence."

Your answer: _____

_____

_____

_____

_____

_____

_____

_____

_____

_____

_____

_____

SUPERVISORY

Tell me about your experience in supervision.

With this broad, open-ended question, the interviewer is listening for pertinent information and how you organize that information. How long have you worked as a supervisor and how many people have you supervised at any given time? What kinds of activities were being performed by your work group and what did you do to contribute to the group's work product? Here is an example, but you will need to tell your own story.

☞ "I have about five years of experience, supervising as many as eight people. We worked closely together to provide high-quality information and customer service to students seeking financial aid at our community college. I established weekly meetings for the staff to provide new information and share solutions to common problems. Once we began working as a team, our speed of processing financial aid packages increased significantly."

Your answer: _____

_____

_____

_____

_____

_____

_____

_____

_____

_____

_____

_____

SUPERVISORY

Tell me how you delegate work effectively.

Think about your leadership qualities because effective delegation is a leadership skill. Add an example if you wish to further clarify your response.

☞ "I trust my employees, so delegation has always been an easy skill for me. When I first begin to manage a team of employees, I watch their job performance to get a clear sense of each person's abilities on the job. I then set professional goals with each one, based on their desire for growth and my observations. This approach allows their readiness for and interest in growth and professional development to dictate my delegation strategy. I also make myself available for questions as they move through their various projects. In my last job, I set regular coaching appointments with several of my employees, while others dropped in more informally."

Your answer: _____

_____

_____

_____

_____

_____

_____

_____

_____

_____

_____

SUPERVISORY

Tell me about a time when you helped in the development of a subordinate.

This is another leadership question. Supervisors who are able to coach their subordinates, lead them to improved performance and everyone wins.

☞ "As the operations manager of a small dental office, I supervised the work of fifteen paraprofessionals and office staff, many of whom were very young and in their first or second job. After each had been on the job for about ninety days, I initiated a short discussion about their goals and the skills they would like to learn or improve. I also provided my input. Out of that came a plan for workplace performance, with goals, a timeline, and a method for evaluation. I coached one particular employee who was able to improve her clinical skill by focusing on practice sessions and asking other technicians for help. At the end of three months, her dentist reported improvement in that skill. In addition, her customer communication skills improved as she became more relaxed in her job."

Your answer: _____

_____

_____

_____

_____

_____

_____

_____

_____

_____

SUPERVISORY

As a supervisor, what do you do when employees working under you don't get along?

Human nature being what it is, there are always a number of situations at work when employees don't get along. Just as you can't pick your relatives, you can't pick your coworkers, either. People see the world differently from each other, have different experiences, and approach problems from different perspectives, resulting in difficult relationships on occasion. You will want to think about your work history and, if possible, choose an experience in which you, as a supervisor, helped with the problem solving that was required.

☞ "In my last job, I supervised a team of twelve people, all of whom had worked for the company for a long time. When I started the job, it was clear to me that two of the team members didn't work well together. I let it go for a couple of weeks, thinking that eventually they would work out their problem, but nothing changed. Finally, I invited both of them to my office and talked with them about a new project we would be starting. I let them know that I felt they would do an excellent job of leading this project, but I had noticed that the communication between them appeared to be impaired. Then, I invited them to find a way to resolve their issue with each other. I made it clear that they would not be invited to lead the new project unless they were willing to move on and, in fact, that their jobs would be in question if they continued to be unwilling to resolve their issue. I also offered to obtain outside assistance for them, if necessary. They apparently talked and found a way to work better with each other. Over the five years I worked with that team, I never again saw any evidence of their conflict."

Your answer: _____

_____

_____

_____

_____

_____

_____

_____

SUPERVISORY

Tell me about a time when you needed to provide corrective feedback about the job performance of someone you supervised.

Think about an experience you had as a supervisor that will fit this question. Remember to provide enough information for the interviewer to understand the situation under which you were providing the feedback, your relationship with that person, the actions you took, and how you contributed to the resulting change in employee behavior. If you were unable to bring about a change in employee behavior, think about another example! Then, think about the performance problem created by the employee's behavior. What did you do to get your point across to the employee? How did you motivate your employee to change that behavior? Were you successful? If not, how did you ultimately resolve the performance issue?

☞ "I remember my first job in supervision. I had a number of young employees, and for many of them, this was their first job. As a result, they didn't understand some of the basic rules of work that most of us take for granted. I remember one young woman who was always late returning from lunch and breaks. I spoke to her about my expectation that she return to work on time. Unfortunately, my casual mention of the situation didn't change her behavior. I documented a couple of examples of continuing lateness, and then asked her to join me in my office at her next work break. I brought up the topic, mentioned the previous conversation, and went over the subsequent examples of continuing lateness. Then I asked her to give me an example of something she expected me to be on time with. Of course, she said it was her paycheck! That discussion brought the point home to her and she was never late returning from lunch again."

Your answer: _____

_____

_____

_____

_____

_____

_____

_____

_____

_____

SUPERVISORY

Describe the circumstances and how you handled firing someone.

Firing someone is a difficult task for most of us. The question here is asking for an example of a time when you did fire an employee. How you handled it becomes important because fired employees can leave employment very negatively and companies do not benefit from the resulting bad-mouthing or the legal complications that can occur when a firing is handled poorly.

☞ "Early on in my last job, I hired a young woman to work at our front desk. While she appeared to learn her duties of answering a multiline telephone, greeting incoming customers, scheduling medical appointments, and coordinating with the back office, she was unable to perform most of her duties without asking several questions, even after a month. We had several conversations about her work performance and what it would take for her to be successful on the job. My assistant provided training on a daily basis, and the new employee appeared to enjoy her work; however, no improvement was noted. All efforts and their results were carefully documented in the employment record. As we came up on the sixty-day probationary employment deadline, I knew that I would need to fire this individual. I met with her, told her again what the front desk job required, and explained that we would be unable to retain her in that job. By the time she had cleared out her desk, she was able to say good-bye to her coworkers."

Your answer: _____

_____

_____

_____

_____

_____

_____

_____

SUPERVISORY

What would you do if a member of your staff seemed upset about something but you didn't know what the problem was about?

It is often difficult to determine how involved in employee problems you, as a supervisor, want to become. The best response is to stick to work problems. To answer this question you will first want to think about the impact the staff member's "upset" is having on the person's work performance. That is what you want to discuss with the staff member directly. Then you can discuss your response to that work problem and your expected outcome. To answer this question, you will want to talk about how you would handle the situation, and discuss the anticipated result of your actions. If you can identify a similar situation that you have experienced, it could be helpful to review that situation and develop your answer from that experience.

☞ "A couple of years ago, one of my staff members seemed to 'disconnect' from her work. By that, I mean that she stopped putting her usual energy into her job, refused projects whenever she could, and started doing the minimum work required. It caught my attention because this employee had always been very invested in her work, willing to help others with projects, and seeing new projects as opportunities to advance her skills. Now she seemed tired a lot, as though she was under a great deal of stress. After a couple of weeks I called her into my office and told her about the change I was seeing in her work behaviors and attitude. I also made it clear that I was concerned about her as an individual and wondered if I could help.

"She told me that her husband was very ill and that the combination of trying to care for him while continuing to work full time was just too much for her to handle. Then we discussed some of her options. She was able to arrange to take a leave of absence for a couple of months, using her leave time and then borrowing from a 'leave bank' that other employees had contributed to in her name. In addition, I encouraged her to talk with her husband's doctor about potential resources she could access to help with her husband's care and her resulting stress. She returned to work after three months. Once again, she was the employee whose work had been so appreciated."

Your answer: _____

_____

_____

_____

_____

_____

CHALLENGES

Tell me about a typical day at your last job.

Few people have a typical day. We all face some unknowns every time we show up for work—something that went wrong, a schedule that changed, a machine that's broken down. Think about your last job and all the primary activities you performed. Make up a typical day, incorporating those activities. Be sure to include a short description of your work and contribution to the overall purpose of your last organization.

☞ "It's hard to describe a typical day because each day on my last job was different, depending on the needs of my clients and the various problems that arose. As the director of financial aid at a community college, I began each day with a short staff meeting. I then reviewed my voice mail and e-mail messages, read my mail, and usually attended another meeting with other directors. We worked for a vice president who was constantly looking for ways to streamline our services and improve accessibility for students. My afternoon often included additional meetings with people inside the institution or in the community, and paperwork. If I was in the office, my afternoons were usually interrupted by frequent questions and problems that needed to be addressed."

Your answer: _____

_____

_____

_____

_____

_____

_____

_____

_____

_____

CHALLENGES

Give me an example of taking care of business day-to-day but also thinking long-range.

Begin by thinking about a long-range goal you had on your last job. How did you reach that goal? How was the day-to-day operation affected by your work to reach the long-term goal? Now you have an example in mind that can be used to answer this question well.

☞ "One of my early jobs was the manager of a Pizza Hut. Some of our business concerns related to the employee costs involved in cleanup at the end of the business day. I was tasked with reducing the time it took to clean both the front and the back of the restaurant, thereby reducing the cost of wages and improving the restaurant's profitability. The short-term goal was to improve the cost effectiveness of the cleanup process. The long-range goal was to systematize the process so it could be maintained in spite of the fairly common employee turnover.

"I began by developing a set of checklists for the servers cleaning the front of the restaurant after closing. Each item was to be checked off and initialed by the person(s) completing the task. A similar checklist was given to the drivers who were responsible for cleaning the back of the restaurant—the kitchen. I pitched in to help with each group's cleaning tasks and was careful to note high-quality performance and extra effort."

Your answer: _____

_____

_____

_____

_____

_____

_____

_____

_____

CHALLENGES

Tell me about the biggest project you've worked on from start to finish.

The word "big" is ambiguous but the biggest project "you've" ever worked on isn't. Whether you were the leader of the effort or not, pick the project to which you made a clearly definable contribution.

☞ "Once, while working for a large school district, we decided to put on a conference for middle school students and their parents to increase their available information about careers and the relationship between jobs and school. An additional goal was to include as many community members in the process as possible to increase the connection between school and community. As we started the planning process and identified our target market, we realized that we had to be prepared for up to 1,000 participants in pairs of two—one parent and one child. When we looked at the content to be included, we identified our purpose as providing assistance with identifying likes and dislikes, exposure to career information, and realization of the opportunities to make choices that were connected to their current education.

"By the time the conference date arrived, we had 968 participants, half of whom took a short, self-scoring interest test; more than 110 presenters in panels and keynote speakers; and a humorist who spoke over lunch. About 50 teachers and school administrators helped with registration and traffic control. Each participating team received a short packet of suggested activities to further investigate their career choices. This was a mammoth project, with many people and pieces of information to be planned, coordinated, and delivered. As the project leader, I was also responsible for resolving conflicts and disagreements among committee members and making sure that everyone was recognized for their various efforts. Upon completion, a report had to be generated to allow other school districts to replicate the project and help us to do it all again next year!"

Your answer: _____

_____

_____

_____

CHALLENGES

Tell me about a project in your last job that you really got excited about.

The most important word in this question is "excited." When you answer, allow yourself to get—and look—excited. Be well enough prepared to have fun with your answer.

☞ "I worked as a sales clerk for a small, family-owned, retail store in a tourist town. By the end of the first month, sales were up and I was given the opportunity to manage the store. It was really fun to reorganize the merchandise to make new products more visible. All items for sale were meticulously cleaned and newly displayed. I rearranged the windows, which hadn't been decorated for years, based on customer demographics and sales records. Sales continued to rise, even after the tourist season was over."

Your answer: _____

_____

_____

_____

_____

_____

_____

_____

_____

_____

_____

_____

142
CHALLENGES

Tell me about the last time you found a creative solution to a problem.

The problem can have occurred at any level of an organization you have worked for in the past, but it is helpful if you can think of a recent example. Frame your answer by starting with some background information about the company and/or problem you are describing. You need to set the stage.

☞ "A store I managed was having a difficult time drawing customers upstairs into the loft area to peruse the merchandise. The loft was important because we needed the floor space and the sales it generated to make the shop profitable. We moved products around, putting the higher-selling ones in the loft in hopes of increasing customer traffic. We tried redoing our signs leading to the upstairs and in the front of the store, without measurable change in sales. Finally, I installed a coffee machine and offered cookies, inviting customers upstairs for a snack. It worked!"

☞ "As a sales representative for the state lottery, I was responsible for the delivery of tickets, point-of-sale equipment and materials, and the security of lottery tickets on display. Many accounts dispensed tickets from their cash registers to maintain security, but the tickets end up scratched and unsellable. The tickets needed to be displayed where customers could be reminded to purchase them. Taking the idea from the cash register tape dispenser, I created a similar device to dispense lottery tickets. It could be attached to the counter with Velcro and the lottery tickets could be rolled up for convenient display. It took up very little counter space. The device was produced out of Plexiglas, so the tickets became their own display."

Your answer: _____

_____

_____

_____

_____

_____

_____

CHALLENGES

Give me an example of a time when you had an idea for improvement and how the company was affected.

You will need to begin by describing the company you are going to talk about as you answer this question. This is a great opportunity for you to talk about an idea you had and acknowledge any contributions of others as part of your success.

☞ "As the new assistant to the vice president of funds acquisition for a child development center, I was tasked with attending and contributing leadership to a group called Women Giving. The group had been in existence for about two years and was designed to raise money for special projects at the center. So far, a project had not been identified and no money had been raised. My goal was to get committee members motivated to move forward.

"I began by listening to the discussion about the kind of project this group wanted to work on. I helped them to specify their interests, researched potential options, and reported back. A coworker suggested that once they picked a project, I could develop a compatible theme for each meeting and bring in a speaker to help the women meet one of their other goals: to have a general educational component at each meeting. Attendance and fund-raising improved."

Your answer: _____

_____

_____

_____

_____

_____

_____

_____

_____

CHALLENGES

Tell me about a time when you used your fact-finding skills to gain information needed to solve a problem.

First, think of an example. It could be a topic you researched, a person you interviewed, telephone calls you made to gather information, or staff in another department with whom you spoke. Your answer should identify the problem to be solved, the methods and types of information you collected to best understand the problem, the information you presented and the format you used, and any recommendations you had.

☞ "I had ordered some materials for a presentation my boss was to make and they didn't come within the time expected. After several phone calls, I was able to locate the person in shipping and receiving who could track our order. Unfortunately, the materials had been sent to the wrong address and never returned. The company sent another set out immediately and we received everything the next day."

Your answer: _____

_____

_____

_____

_____

_____

_____

_____

_____

_____

_____

CHALLENGES

You have just returned from vacation. Your boss has scheduled an important meeting at 10:00, a large customer has left a message indicating that a problem must be resolved this morning, and the sales department needs a proposal from you by 11:00. How will you respond?

My first, gut-level response might be, "Well, how did they ever get by without me while I was on vacation?" Suppress that response! Instead, think about your company's expectations for setting priorities and multitasking.

☞ "I would talk with my boss to see if the meeting was more important than the client or the sales proposal. If the boss felt that his meeting could wait, I would handle the large customer first, delegating as much of the sales proposal as possible until I could finalize it before the 11:00 deadline. If, on the other hand, the boss felt that his meeting took precedence over all else, I would delegate the customer problem and the proposal—after all, someone was doing these things while I was on vacation—and keep the boss happy."

Your answer: _____

_____

_____

_____

_____

_____

_____

_____

_____

_____

CHALLENGES

Tell me about a time when you had to juggle priorities to meet a deadline.

The interviewer will be specific, so you should also be specific. Don't simply reply with, "My job requires this every day." The interviewer is generally seeking information on past experiences, which are indicators of future performance. If you saved your previous employer money, you will probably do the same for your new employer.

If you are good at something, always try to prove it with a story. An example is much better than a simple statement. Remember STAR—Describe the Situation or Task, the Action You Took, and Results Achieved.

☞ "Just yesterday, my boss handed me a project that was more important than anything else on my desk. I set aside two competing deadlines and began work on the new project. I had to skip lunch and work two hours of overtime, but I met the deadline for the meeting next morning."

Your answer: _____

_____

_____

_____

_____

_____

_____

_____

_____

_____

_____

_____

CHALLENGES

Describe a time when you had to make an unpopular decision or announcement.

Most of us prefer not to have to make unpopular decisions which, by their very nature, are, well . . . unpopular. Be sure to include information about how you addressed any fallout from the decision's announcement.

☞ "In my last position, I was a department manager for a large company. A long-term, valued employee became ill. Although he tried to continue working, pain medication and fatigue levels eventually caused him to take a leave of absence. We held his job for one year, using temporary workers to perform his job duties. At the end of the year, the employee's medical condition hadn't changed significantly and he continued to receive disability payments. His insurance company started discussing long-term disability benefits, and return to work in the foreseeable future was clearly not expected. To complicate matters, our company had a new contract and the vacant position really needed to be filled with someone we could count on. After many discussions and much thought, I recommended that we dismiss the employee and hire someone in his position. It was the best decision for the company but clearly not a popular decision with my employees."

Your answer: _____

_____

_____

_____

_____

_____

_____

_____

_____

_____

CHALLENGES

Tell me about the last time you went over budget.

Make sure you can explain how the situation was resolved and what you learned from the example you use to answer this question. Avoid selecting an example that would be so major that it had a long-term negative effect on your employer's ability to conduct business, caused the company to file for bankruptcy, or made the company go under.

☞ "Once, while working for an extended care facility as the operations manager, a new facility opened its doors. All of their staff members wore new, carefully maintained uniforms. After a couple of weeks, we began to receive comments from visitors about our lack of uniforms. We researched costs and decided to buy uniforms to maintain our market share. I was in charge of the project. Unfortunately, the estimates I was given did not include the night shift. When the uniforms had been purchased, the result was lowered staffing patterns for two subsequent months. All the administrators had to work overtime. I never forgot the lesson. Now, when I am in charge of a project, I put several checks and balances in place and go over the budget more than once. I have not failed to bring a project to completion under or at budget since that experience."

Your answer: _____

_____

_____

_____

_____

_____

_____

_____

_____

_____

CHALLENGES

Tell me about one of your projects that failed.

We all have projects that fail—but that doesn't make them easy to talk about, especially in an interview. Think about a project that went poorly and make sure you include information about what you learned and/or changed to make sure it didn't happen again. Don't respond with a large, failed project that cost the company a significant amount of dollars.

☞ "I worked for a landscape contractor while I was in college. The first project I worked for him went well, and I returned to the shop ready to go out on the next assignment. Before I got there, the customer had called with several complaints about the way that I had left the work site. I left out her hose and hadn't cleaned the grass clippings off the walks. She was very angry about the things I had seen as minor. From the customer's perspective, her project had failed and I learned to look at all of my projects from the customer's perspective before I considered them done."

☞ "For about five years, I was self-employed. My business produced small, personal care products. I worked the business part-time before I left my job and made it my full-time business. We did well for a couple of years. When my suppliers raised their prices, I raised my prices to compensate for the higher costs. However, I didn't have the marketing experience to be able to increase my customer base, so the business folded six months later. I learned that, to make a business successful, you need to have all of the skills required or the resources to hire people who have the skills you lack."

Your answer: _____

_____

_____

_____

_____

_____

_____

_____

INFLUENCE/CONVINCE

Describe a time when you had to persuade someone to accept your point of view. How were you successful?

Think about both the information you collected that served as a foundation for your argument and the strategy you used to persuade someone to support your point of view. Don't appear to "strong arm" or bully the person you are trying to persuade.

☞ "As a marketing person for a large school district, I was asked to review the dropout program to see if I could make any recommendations to improve the number of referrals into the program and the success rate of student participation. As I began my research, I met with the Dropout Initiative Committee and listened to their thoughts. I then looked at a demographic profile of students who had dropped out over the last calendar year. I identified several factors that would need to be addressed to increase self-referral or agency referral into the program. Several cultural factors—such as family need for income from the student and language barriers—were included. I also noted that many dropouts and their families did not see education as a tangible product, so increasing their understanding of the connection between school and work would be helpful.

"Some of the school board members didn't agree with my assessment. However, as I presented my data and answered their questions, I could feel their interest increasing and their willingness to learn improving. Eventually, after much discussion, they agreed to let me proceed to develop the materials and guidelines necessary to market the dropout program in the ways I was recommending. It was so exciting to successfully persuade the board to my point of view."

Your answer: _____

_____

_____

_____

_____

_____

DRIVE/SUCCESS

You are working on your business degree at a local college, and you work as a waiter at night to pay your tuition. How could you implement at work what you are learning in class?

This question hits a lot of bases. It can provide the interviewer with information about how you prioritize, manage your time, handle stress, and how you address multiple—and sometimes competing—tasks. All that information can be given while you are answering the question about applying school to work.

☞ "I'm learning how to manage a business, but as a waiter, I don't own my own business or have any control over the business, per se. However, I do have control over myself and how I choose to view my work. So, I can act like I own the business, like an entrepreneur. I could go out and have some inexpensive business cards printed with my name and cell phone number, and I would give them to my customers, telling them to call me ahead of time and I'd be sure they got a good table. I could buy some inexpensive cut flowers from Sam's Club and give individual blossoms to the ladies at my tables. I'd make sure I always had a lighter in my pocket in case someone needed a cigarette lit. I'd go out of my way to remember customers' names and keep a little black book to remind me of details, so I could make my customers feel special. I bet I would have every table filled every night and make more tips than any waiter in that restaurant."

Your answer: _____

_____

_____

_____

_____

_____

_____

_____

_____

DRIVE/SUCCESS

Tell me about the last time you saved the company money.

Saving the company money could have occurred because of some direct action you took as outlined in the example that follows. It could have been the result of information you gathered or an option you generated that a boss took forward. Either way, make sure that your contribution is well defined.

☞ "As you probably noticed on my résumé, I worked for a small nutraceutical company as operations manager for five years. We had received our primary product from the same supplier for a number of years and our retail price was based on our supplier's cost. When we received a solicitation from one of their competitors, I decided to research other companies who had the capacity to meet our needs. Working with the owners, we identified another supplier, conducted the necessary clinical studies, and found that we could reduce our costs by 30 percent. The change in supplier not only saved my employer money but allowed the company to offer our customers some special deals, as well."

Your answer: _____

_____

_____

_____

_____

_____

_____

_____

_____

_____

_____

DRIVE/SUCCESS

Describe a specific example of a time when you took the initiative.

The interviewer wants to see if you can take charge of a situation and make decisions on your own without waiting to be told to do something. Taking the initiative also displays your leadership capabilities.

☞ "My boss was out of the office one afternoon, and I took a call from a particularly difficult customer. She was in a lot of pain and her order of medications had not arrived. When I checked the computer, her shipment had not been sent, even though the system showed the order had been received. I apologized to the customer and made the decision to FedEx the order overnight, at no extra cost to the customer. When my boss returned the next morning, I explained the problem, and he agreed with my decision. I had saved a valuable customer from suffering undue pain and righted a wrong that was clearly our shipping department's fault, all at minimal cost to my company."

Your answer: _____

_____

_____

_____

_____

_____

_____

_____

_____

_____

_____

INDUSTRY

Why do you want to work in this industry?

Your research and knowledge of your own job history should provide you with the answer to this question. The information you need falls into three areas: 1. What about the industry has your interest? 2. What jobs in your history led you to this industry? 3. If you do not have any experience in this industry, what skills did you use in previous jobs that will be similar to the skills you will need in this job? The new industry may interest you now because of non-work exposure (volunteer or hobby interests) and your skills will transfer.

☞ "As you know from my résumé, I have eight years of experience in training. While working in the airline industry will be new for me, I have experience in other customer service settings that will transfer into the new job. In addition, I have been a licensed pilot for the last ten years, so I am familiar with the terminology, and I am excited to get to work in the airline industry."

Your answer: _____

_____

_____

_____

_____

_____

_____

_____

_____

_____

_____

INDUSTRY

What important trends do you see in our industry?

Without research, you can't answer this question, so do your homework. You should have information about trends in the industry and have thought about how you can help the new company take advantage of those trends.

☞ "One primary trend I see across our industry is the increase in the need for mechanics with customer service skills. While the front office used to work closely with our customers and mechanics stayed in the shop, we are coming to expect that mechanics will be directly involved with the customer. They need to be able to answer questions in language the customer can understand, respond to customer questions, and manage conflict in addition to being very good mechanics. Their written communication skills must be good as well, because their paperwork needs to be accurate and complete."

Your answer: _____

_____

_____

_____

_____

_____

_____

_____

_____

_____

_____

_____

INDUSTRY

Who are our three major competitors? What advantages do you think they might have over us?

Your research into the industry should have provided you with information about the company's competitors. You will want to identify the competitors, talk about their strengths, and tell how you could help to reduce at least one of their advantages or improve one of your company's weaknesses.

☞ "Your three primary competitors are Coca-Cola, Pepsi, and the generic products sold by supermarkets. The first two have worldwide markets, have high name recognition, and spend large budgets on marketing. Store brands have low cost in their favor. Your product seems more appropriate to a niche market for energy drinks, where it won't compete directly with the giant companies. The question then becomes how to go about getting the word out to our potential customers. Money spent in accumulating specific information about customer demographics, interests, behavioral patterns, and psychographics can help you focus on your market. While I have expertise in all of those areas, my last three years have been spent in psychographics. That is where I can offer your company the greatest advantages."

Your answer: _____

_____

_____

_____

_____

_____

_____

_____

_____

_____

COMPANY

What do you know about our company? How did you get that information?

Research, research, research before the interview. The more you know about the company, the more interested you appear to the interviewer. **Every** subject matter expert we interviewed said that one of the key factors in selecting candidates was their knowledge of the company. They all expected intelligent questions from interviewees relating to the company's business and products and how the candidate will contribute in the new position. The purpose of asking how you gained that information is to determine how you gather facts before making decisions and solving problems, and what you know about using technology (i.e., the Internet) to conduct research.

Answer the question by focusing on a brief review of the company's history, its key products, its place in the market, its mission, culture, and financial position. Don't go into too much detail. Keep this part of your answer short. Then move on to the challenges the company faces in a fast-moving market and how it compares to its competitors.

☞ "MCI is one of the world's largest providers of IP technology solutions, including business data, Internet, network, and voice services. It was founded in 1968 as a public company whose stock is traded on the NYSE. Even though WorldCom purchased MCI in the late 1990s, the name was recently changed back to MCI in response to the controversy surrounding the accounting fraud and resulting bankruptcy filing in 2002. I was very impressed that MCI was able to work itself out of a Chapter 11 and continue to provide the diversity of services for which it has always been known.

In my research findings, I related most to MCI's values to serve its customers with innovation, value, and integrity. It is that philosophy that will help MCI overcome the negative press it has experienced between 2002 and 2005. It is your dedication to putting the customer first that attracts me most to this job. I trained more than 200 customer service representatives at my current employer in providing WOW! customer service, which improved satisfaction ratings by 150 percent. I am confident I could help MCI in the same way."

☞ "I gained my information by carefully reviewing your corporate Web site. I went on to read stories in Forbes and Fortune magazines, and I checked the SEC's Web site to get an outside perspective of the scandal. Hoovers.com helped me understand your current financial position and standing."

Your answer: _____

_____

_____

_____

_____

COMPANY

What do you think is our organization's strength?

Again, research, research, and research. This question is your opportunity to shine. Demonstrate your knowledge and motivation by giving an answer that shows your understanding of this company's source of pride. It could be a product, service, their research, attention to details, or ability to market their products successfully. This is a specific question, so it deserves a specific answer.

☞ "Your people are your greatest strength. From my research, I have learned that your organization hires well, paying attention to the skills needed in the job now and the skills you anticipate will be needed in the near future. Your workforce receives regular training to maintain their expertise and you place high importance on communication, both within the organization and externally."

Your answer: _____

_____

_____

_____

_____

_____

_____

_____

_____

_____

_____

COMPANY

What do you think our number one priority should be?

Get as much information about the company as you can before you prepare an answer to this question. You want to identify a priority and what you can do to enhance the company in that area.

☞ "You have excellent products, but products don't continue to sell if you don't provide high-quality customer service. You have a great reputation at this time, which is why I am interested in working for you. Your customer service department could benefit from some standardization of its processes and paperwork so the same high-quality interaction that you currently have with your customers can continue as the company grows. My experience in niche marketing with medium-sized companies could really benefit your company in this area."

Your answer: _____

_____

_____

_____

_____

_____

_____

_____

_____

_____

_____

_____

160

COMPANY

What would you do differently if you ran the company?

Be careful not to be too critical when you answer this question. The idea is to demonstrate your ability to contribute to the company, not to run the company down. Choose something about the company that your efforts could help to improve.

☞ "Your company has become very successful in a short period of time, which is one of the qualities that attracts me here. When I visited your Web page, I noticed that most of your success is related to products developed to address one disease. What happens if a cure is found? I would do some research into other medical conditions that could be alleviated by the same or similar products to what you already produce. In addition, I would begin an effort to look into the development of other products that take advantage of the niche marketing you already do. For example, are there other medicinal products that could use the same basic materials and appeal to your current market? My background in pharmaceutical research could help you in both of those areas."

Your answer: _____

_____

_____

_____

_____

_____

_____

_____

_____

_____

_____

COMPANY

Why do you want to work here?

The interviewer is asking for specific information that you should have gathered in your research. The information you provide could be about the company, the position for which you are applying, or include information about both.

☞ "I am interested in working for this school district for a couple of reasons. First, you have a reputation for high-quality education. Your students perform well on national tests, several win community awards, and your graduation rate is high. Second, this position would give me the opportunity to expand my own skills. In addition to teaching social studies, I could sponsor student council activities and work with other clubs. I already have some ideas for building leadership skills in the students through their club activities."

Your answer: _____

_____

_____

_____

_____

_____

_____

_____

_____

_____

_____

COMPANY

In what specific ways will our company benefit from hiring you?

This is another opportunity to talk about your strengths, but be specific. Also, note the question asks for "ways," plural. Be prepared to discuss how you will help the company move forward in accordance with its goals.

☞ "You are looking for a sales representative who will work well in an environment where continuous improvement is expected. In my last position, I was able to develop a new device for hanging point-of-sale materials that cut the time necessary to install the materials and guaranteed they would stay in place. I also was instrumental in creating several sales tracking forms that our customers really liked. Your company will benefit from this experience as I find more efficient ways to support your sales processes."

Your answer: _____

_____

_____

_____

_____

_____

_____

_____

_____

_____

_____

_____

PRODUCTS AND SERVICES

If you had the opportunity to develop a new product or service to add to our line, what would it be?

This is another of those questions where you can make a suggestion without managing to insult the new company or be negative. Your answer depends on how much you know about the industry, the company where you are applying, their product line, and their options for new products. In a service industry, you need the same information about new services that could benefit their customers.

☞ "As your chef, I would redevelop some of our sauces for lighter options. More flavor and fewer fats have become increasingly popular among our clientele, making those options more important to your restaurant's continuing success."

☞ "As a member of your leadership team at South Central Healthcare, I would want to get more information about your current clients and the services they would like to see added before answering this question effectively. Even without that knowledge, I believe the addition of some ancillary services, radiology, and expanded laboratory processes would make us a one-stop medical clinic, benefiting both our patients and our bottom line."

Your answer: _____

_____

_____

_____

_____

_____

_____

_____

_____

_____

PRODUCTS AND SERVICES

When and how have you seen or used our product(s) or service(s)? What did you like or not like about them?

The interviewer is trying to discover just how much research you conducted before coming to the interview. Do you know exactly what the company sells? How much do you know about the industry in general and competitive products and/or services? Are you excited about them? How is your enthusiasm level? Do you have enough insight into these products or services to make recommendations for improvement so the company can become more competitive?

☞ "I was in the market for a new car last year, and I test drove several Honda models. I was so impressed with the CR-V's handling that I ended up purchasing one, even though a Nissan Murano had been my first choice. According to <u>Consumer Reports</u>, your safety record is the best in the industry, and your SUVs have the lowest rollover rate I've seen compared to your competitors. For a new-car sales representative, that's a great advantage. I am confident I'll become one of your top sales reps."

Your answer: _____

_____

_____

_____

_____

_____

_____

_____

_____

_____

_____

_____

POSITION

What do you know about the position for which you are applying?

Put together any information that you have been able to gather from the job description or ad that you saw on the job. If you are lucky enough to know someone who works for the company, you might also conduct a short interview to gather information about the reporting structure for the position. Look for anything about the job's responsibilities, place in the organization, number of people supervised (if any), and level of decision making. If you don't know much about the job, now is the time to ask.

☞ "I understand only what I read in the job announcement. I would be responsible for supervising the nursing staff. I know that you have several clinics, covering about one hundred square miles, so I would do some traveling to visit those clinics and see the clinical managers in their settings. I will need to keep current on medical issues and ensure all nurses receive the training necessary for them to do their best work. There is much that I don't know about the job—for example, my relationship to the physicians who work here and my responsibility for direct patient relations."

Your answer: _____

_____

_____

_____

_____

_____

_____

_____

_____

_____

_____

_____

POSITION

Why do you want this job?

Answer this question with enthusiasm and confidence. Leave no doubt in the interviewer's mind that you really want this job and that it's a perfect match with your short-term and long-term goals. Do your research before the interview so you know as many details as possible about the position for which you are applying. Besides the classified ad, go to the company's Web site and search their career pages for the full job description. If you can't find it there, call the HR department and request that the job description be e-mailed or faxed to you before the interview.

Whatever you do, don't answer this question with desperation. For example, "Well, if I don't get this job, I'm going to lose my house and my wife is going to divorce me." Yikes! The interviewer is probably thinking, "This person is desperate for **any** job. If I hire him, he'll probably leave to find his true passion as soon as he pays his bills. There isn't much of a chance that this will be a long-term relationship."

Also, don't focus on what the company can do for you: "You have great benefits and one of the highest wages in the city." Instead, answer the question with what you can do for the company and how well the job fits with your experience and abilities.

☞ "I have been following your company in the news over the past year and noticed that you are creating a new customer relationship management system. When I saw your advertisement for a software developer, I knew that I would be able to contribute significantly to your new product line right away. At XYZ Company, I wrote the code for a similar database using Oracle and finished the project two weeks ahead of the deadline."

Your answer: _____

_____

_____

_____

_____

_____

_____

_____

_____

_____

_____

_____

POSITION

How is your experience relevant to this job?

Review your current job description and the description of the job for which you are applying. Look for similarities in tasks and skills. You will want to draw those comparisons for your interviewer.

☞ "As a computer teacher in my last position, I worked with students to integrate technology into their studies. I collaborated with other teachers to assist them in using technology in each of their classrooms. I was instrumental in receiving a grant to fund modular technology to increase student and teacher access. Serving as your school district's technology officer will make good use of the skills I built on my last job."

Your answer: _____

_____

_____

_____

_____

_____

_____

_____

_____

_____

_____

POSITION

If you are hired, what do you plan to do in the first week/month on the job?

If you have been able to gather enough information about the company and the job during your research, you might be able to make some decisions ahead of time about what you would do within the first few weeks on the job. The reality is that you generally need to be on the job a month or so before you will uncover the real problems that need to be fixed.

☞ "I feel it's wise to spend the first month or so on a new job observing the work teams, getting to know the company's policies and procedures, and researching the decisions my predecessor made. I want to make sure that I truly understand the group's dynamics before I begin making any changes."

Your answer: _____

_____

_____

_____

_____

_____

_____

_____

_____

_____

_____

_____

POSITION

What would you like to accomplish in your first year if we hire you?

Your interviewer doesn't expect you to have a perfect answer to this question. The most important thing is that you try to answer it. Otherwise, you appear to be reticent, unwilling to cooperate, and/or not very creative. Answering this question as best you can tells the interviewer a lot about how you think, how you communicate, and whether you can forecast and plan.

☞ "I read the recent <u>Business Journal</u> article on your proposed expansion into commercial construction. You have more than 25 years of experience building homes in our area, and I've heard many good things about the quality of your construction. That's one of the reasons I was attracted by your advertisement for a commercial superintendent. If I understand your plans, you need contractors that include experienced carpenters and other tradespeople who can maintain your high-quality reputation. I have a network of craftsmen in our area that will allow me to pick and choose the best people for the job. Besides staffing, I see the need for extensive business development among local developers. I may recommend that we hire a full-time account executive who can call on every developer in the city and attend industry association meetings. At the end of my first year on the job, I would expect this new division to add 20 percent to our existing annual revenue."

Your answer: _____

_____

_____

_____

_____

_____

_____

_____

_____

_____

POSITION

If you could, what would you change about this position?

It's not really your job to change the position. It's your job to make sure you fit the job description. Until you have been in the position for a while, you aren't qualified to make decisions about what to change, anyway.

☞ "I wouldn't change anything at the moment. I won't know enough about the job's problems to recommend changes until I've been on the job for a while. I need to know more about my role in the department, how well the person I am replacing did his or her job, and how the team members work together. Once I get some experience under my belt, I will be able to make recommendations."

Your answer: _____

_____

_____

_____

_____

_____

_____

_____

_____

_____

171
PERFECT JOB

How would you describe your ideal work environment? What environments allow you to be especially effective?

Think about all of the environments in which you have worked. Have you been in a production setting, an office setting, or spent much of your time in a car? What about these settings have been conducive to your accomplishment of work? Next, think about the setting in which the new job would occur. Answer this question with a cross between the two and talk about your ability to adapt to most situations.

☞ "I have worked in a cubicle and enclosed offices in the past, using both environments very effectively. However, I find my best work is done in a mixture of shared and private space. When I work on a joint project or some kind of problem solving, the ideas and comments of others energize me. Their feedback generates new ways of thinking and new options to consider, improving my thinking process and the resulting product. When I write reports, I prefer a quiet space where I can concentrate on the work at hand. Based on my previous experience, I can be flexible enough to adapt to most work environments."

Your answer: _____

_____

_____

_____

_____

_____

_____

_____

_____

_____

_____

_____

172
PERFECT JOB

Describe your ideal company to work for.

Hopefully, your research will have produced some information about the company's culture and organizational structure. You want to speak to your ideals in a workplace, while at the same time being general enough to remain in consideration for the job. Some company characteristics include treatment of employees, interest in providing opportunities for advancement, customer focus and orientation to customer service, training focus, involvement in the community, emphasis on team or individual contribution, and quality of the physical plant as a work environment, among others. Reading the mission/vision/values statements of the company is a good place to start.

☞ "My ideal company is one with high ethical standards. Because the federal government often funds the work I do, I am careful to keep a close watch on our budgets and our objectives. I appreciate a team focus, clear communication within the organization, and high standards for customer service. In addition, a work environment suitable to maintaining confidentiality would be important."

Your answer: _____

_____

_____

_____

_____

_____

_____

_____

_____

_____

_____

173
PERFECT JOB

If we hire you, what aspect of this job do you think you'll like best?

You can't answer this question unless you know something about the job. You can get some of the information you need from the job posting or advertisement. If that isn't enough, then you should respond to this question with one of your own.

☞ "Can you give me more details about what this job entails? Your advertisement was too general for me to answer your question without more information."

When you have the info you need, then select the most important aspect of the job as what you like best.

☞ "I like interfacing with constituents the best. As with any government PR position, building awareness of the candidate's platform requires getting the message to the people. I look forward to the opportunity of working with you to help define that message and then finding innovative ways to convince the citizens of your district that you are the right person for the position."

Your answer: _____

_____

_____

_____

_____

_____

_____

_____

174
PERFECT JOB

What aspects of this job will you like least?

This is a hard question to answer. While you want to be honest, you also don't want to provide an answer that will keep you from being hired. The best strategy is to identify some facet of your job duties that can occur in any job you might apply for and talk about what you learned.

☞ "The job you are offering meets many of my needs. It will give me the opportunity to further develop my skills and expand my professional opportunities, which is the reason I am so interested. Because I am not in the job at this time, my knowledge of what it entails is limited. I can, however, speak to job duties I have performed in the past that have not been among my favorite tasks. For example, attending meetings that are not well organized and do not have productive results will stretch my patience. As a result, I try to take some responsibility for asking about the goals of meetings I attend and do my part to reach those goals."

Your answer: _____

_____

_____

_____

_____

_____

_____

_____

_____

_____

_____

175
TRAVEL

How does the frequent travel required for this job fit into your lifestyle?

Advertisements for jobs that require travel often state as much and some jobs just naturally require travel, so you should be prepared for this question if you are applying for such a job. You want to assure your interviewer that your lifestyle can accommodate being away from home frequently. Be careful, however, not to give away too much personal information that can set you up for discrimination. For instance, letting your interviewer know now that you have a disabled husband and ten kids at home would not be a wise move! On the other hand, if you are single with no encumbrances, then it could be to your advantage to mention it.

☞ "I look forward to the frequent travel required for this job. My family is fully behind my career goals and has become accustomed to my traveling often as part of my current job."

☞ "My lifestyle is all about travel, even outside of work. I thoroughly enjoy exploring new places and meeting new people. When a job allows me to combine that pleasure with work, then it's even better. I'm single, so I have no problems with being on the road a lot."

Your answer: _____

_____

_____

_____

_____

_____

_____

_____

_____

_____

_____

_____

176
TRAVEL

You don't live in the community where you will be working. How will the commute affect your work?

Commuting takes time and energy away from the rest of your life, including your work life. Experts on stress management often recommend that you use your time to and from work to gear up and de-stress. Make sure your answer is well-rounded.

☞ "I have commuted to work several times in the past, and although it takes more time out of my day, I find that time useful in dealing with my stress. I will use the time coming and going from work to process my thoughts regarding the day's work and gearing up for the day to come. One technique I use to increase the effectiveness of my commute is to keep a small tape player in my car. As ideas occur to me, I can tape them and save the thoughts for my return to work. When I find that I just need to unwind, I rent books on CD or simply listen to music. On days that I work overtime, I have friends in the community with whom I can stay."

Your answer: _____

_____

_____

_____

_____

_____

_____

_____

_____

_____

_____

177
COMPANY CULTURE

Our company believes that employees should give time back to the community. How do you feel about that?

If you are a community volunteer, this is a question you hope the interviewer will ask. If not, you could think about community activities you could be interested in performing and compose your answer around those activities. Another answer to this question could be to ask more questions to make sure you understand the company's philosophy about "giving back to the community." Some companies hold community service in such high regard that they have a full-time community coordinator position in their workforce.

☞ "I have always volunteered at a couple of community agencies. Currently, I help with reading at our library, and I volunteer once a month at our elementary school. In addition, I have participated in the community cleanup campaign for the past three years and really enjoy that experience."

☞ "I have been very busy raising a family over the last two years, so my community activities have been restricted to participating at my child's school. As my daughter gets older, I expect to be more involved."

☞ "I really enjoy participating in community volunteer activities. Tell me a little about your policy to support employee participation."

Your answer: _____

_____

_____

_____

_____

_____

_____

_____

_____

_____

178
COMPANY CULTURE

What would you say if I told you that you were giving a poor interview today?

Your first reaction might be, "Poor, by what standards?" However, that is probably not the best answer to this question. This question is designed to shock you to see what kind of a reaction the interviewer gets back from you. In many ways, the question is very much like any question designed to place you under stress. First, suppress that "personal attack" reaction. Instead, develop an attitude of curiosity. Your best response is to ask questions.

☞ "Well, that doesn't sound good for us if we are both hoping to find a match in this job. What makes you see my interview as a poor one?"

If you get an answer, you will then have some information to respond to. What's most important is that you don't react defensively. Take the question as a challenge!

Your answer: _____

_____

_____

_____

_____

_____

_____

_____

_____

_____

_____

COMPANY CULTURE

I have interviewed several people for this job. Why should I hire you?

This can be seen as a trick question because you don't know who else the company is interviewing. Use that to your advantage by acknowledging that you don't know your competition's skills and then talk about your skills. In addition, add a little information about your personal characteristics.

☞ "I don't know anything about the other people you are interviewing for this job, but I can tell you why you should hire me. I have exactly the skills you need for this job.

- I can meet deadlines.
- I have strong communication skills.
- I can be flexible in problem solving to get the desired results.
- I enjoy performing this work. As a result, I am easy to work with.
- I enjoy producing a team product and look forward to being highly productive.
- I can type 90 words per minute and am proficient in MS Word.
- I have more than five years of supervisory experience.
- I noticed in my research that your company functions in a team environment, and I work well on a team.
- Because your company…
- I meet all of the qualifications you have outlined in your advertisement at careerbuilder.com, plus…"

Your answer: _____

_____

_____

_____

_____

_____

_____

_____

WORKING HOURS

When would you be available?

Always give your current employer adequate notice before leaving. If you agree to stop working tomorrow so that you are available instantly, your interviewer will assume you would do the same to his or her company in the future. Your employer always needs time to find a replacement or transition your work to someone else in the company in the meantime. Show enthusiasm for the new job, though, and let the interviewer see and feel how interested you are.

☞ "I am really excited to begin this new job, but I need to train someone to take my place in my current job first. I would want to give my current employer at least two weeks' notice. Will that be okay?"

☞ "When will you be ready for me? Because I was laid off from my last job during a company downsizing, I am available immediately. I can't wait to plunge into this new responsibility. It's exciting!"

Your answer: _____

_____

_____

_____

_____

_____

_____

_____

_____

_____

WORKING HOURS

How flexible are your working hours?

"As flexible as they need to be," is the natural response. It's the opposite response that you need to worry about. You need to be careful about revealing too much about religious obligations or family problems that might limit the days and/or number of hours you can work. You don't want to set yourself up for discrimination. Don't tell your interviewer that you aren't available in the evenings because you are a single parent and have two children who need you. Don't explain a health problem that limits the amount of stress you can endure. And especially don't mention your religious affiliation.

☞ "I'm not sure what type of time commitment you are expecting for this position, but I am generally flexible when it comes to working hours. I work one weekend every four weeks for my current employer, and I have been known to work overtime to get a project done on time."

Your answer: _____

_____

_____

_____

_____

_____

_____

_____

_____

_____

_____

_____

WORKING HOURS

Each employee in this department works overtime one weekend a month. How do you feel about that?

If you have done your homework and every employee in the department works overtime, you will probably know that going into the interview. As long as you are willing to work overtime, this should be an easy question to answer. There are times that an inexperienced interviewer will use this question to try to determine your religious preferences. In that case, the question is illegal. Answer the question as if the interviewer did not have that intention.

☞ "Overtime is a fact of life in every job I have ever had, sometimes including evenings as well as weekends. I work long hours when the job requires it."

Your answer: _____

_____

_____

_____

_____

_____

_____

_____

_____

_____

_____

_____

_____

_____

SALARY

What do you expect your starting salary to be?

Talk about a trick question! It is always to your advantage to let the employer tell you the salary range first. Try not to be the first one to name a salary or hourly rate. Instead, here are some questions you could ask to get more information and a comment you could make.

☞ "What is the salary range for similar jobs in your company?"

☞ "What do you typically pay someone with my background?"

☞ "I'm sure we can agree on a reasonable amount when the time comes."

Be prepared by knowing the going rate for your position in your geographical area and your bottom line (walk-away point). There are many salary research sites on the Internet that offer this type of information so you can be prepared. If you must answer this question with a number, state a range rather than a specific amount.

☞ "My understanding is that a job like the one you are describing may be in the range of $_____."

Your answer: _____
_____
_____
_____
_____
_____
_____
_____
_____

SALARY

The salary you are asking for is near the top of the range for this job. Why should we pay you this much?

The reason they should pay you this much is because you and your skills are worth it! This question is really just another way of asking, "Why should we hire you?" Think about what sets you apart from others who may be seeking this job. What special knowledge, experiences, personal qualities, or skills do you bring to this job that will enhance the company? Do your research so you can identify one of your strengths that will benefit the company.

☞ "I know that you have an international workforce and I spent a number of years living outside of the United States, so I look forward to working with people of different cultures. I also speak Spanish as well as English."

☞ "I know that your primary customers are governmental agencies within the defense industry. I have experience working with federal and state agencies and feel very comfortable working with their staffs."

☞ "The job we are discussing will take fine attention to detail skills and I am very good at that. As a book-keeper in my previous job, I was able to balance the business books every month. People would make errors throughout the month by entering sales receipts incorrectly or miscalculating an account payable. I was always able to find and correct the mistakes before the books went to our accountant."

Your answer: _____

_____

_____

_____

_____

_____

_____

_____

_____

_____

SALARY

Why would you consider a cut in pay to take this job?

If you are applying for a job that you have researched, you will already know that a pay cut is necessary for you to get the job. As a result, you will probably have decided to take the pay cut, rather than being surprised by this question. There are several reasons any of us might take a cut in pay for a specific job opportunity. Here are some good reasons for you to consider.

☞ "Money is not a primary motivator for me. This job offers me the opportunity to…"

☞ "In addition to pay, several of your benefits including your liberal vacation policies and health insurance coverage make up the difference in pay for me."

☞ "I expected to take a small cut in pay to generate the job opportunity I am interested in."

Some poor answers to this question would be:

☞ "I have been looking for work for a long time and will take anything at this point."

☞ "My previous company laid me off and this is the best I can do."

Your answer: _____

_____

_____

_____

_____

_____

_____

_____

_____

Puzzles, Riddles, and Brain Teasers

Puzzles, riddles, brain teasers, and impossible questions have been around as long as the Silicon Valley. They reflect the belief that employees in high-tech industries must constantly question assumptions, think on their feet, and see things from a unique perspective. These difficult questions are supposed to test those abilities. Over the years, mainstream industries have picked up on these questions, so it shouldn't surprise you if you are asked one or two during an interview. The more important creative thinking is in your job, the more likely that you will be asked to solve a puzzle or riddle or answer an impossible question.

It would take an entire book to deal with every question you might be asked, and every one of them will be difficult to answer. The reality is that there is often no "right" answer to many of these questions. The point is to see how you handle difficult situations (i.e., stress) and whether you can think "outside the box."

Most of these questions require that you communicate your thinking process and not just deliver an answer. It is more about your approach to solving the problem than it is about the answer itself. Don't harangue your interviewer with questions during the process, though. Consider this a monologue, not a dialogue.

The correct answer (when there is a correct one) is probably simple, but it is rarely the first answer that comes to your mind. You are better off if you can come up with an answer other than the one listed here. Your interviewer will be more likely to remember you if you are unique!

PUZZLES, RIDDLES, AND BRAIN TEASERS

How long would it take to move Pikes Peak?

A version of this question (with Mount Fuji instead of Pikes Peak) supposedly originated with the consulting firm Booz, Allen and Hamilton. The correct answer would be a mathematical equation, so if you are thus inclined, you could use a Fermi estimation. For those of us less mathematically endowed, there are more general answers that won't require advanced math and allow you to interject a bit of humor.

☞ "That would depend on how many people and how much equipment were assigned to the task. Much of the mountain is made up of granite, so you would need lots of dynamite. For a single person with a spoon, it would take billions of days. For the entire population of Colorado using the largest dump trucks made, it would take years. At least you wouldn't need supplemental oxygen if you used Colorado residents!"

Your answer: _____

_____

_____

_____

_____

_____

_____

_____

_____

_____

_____

PUZZLES, RIDDLES, AND BRAIN TEASERS

Why are manhole covers round?

This question is often attributed to Microsoft, but it actually first appeared in 1983 in a book by Martin Gardner that collected <u>Scientific American</u> columns back to the early 1970s. Even Gardner admits he didn't invent the question. This question has become so common now that Microsoft no longer asks it, but other companies still do. There are many possible answers to this question, the most common of which appears first on the back of this card.

☞ "Manhole covers are round because a cover of any other shape could fall into its hole and get lost or injure someone. A round cover has the same diameter in all directions, so it will never fall into the hole."

☞ "Manhole covers are round because they are easier to transport. They can be rolled."

☞ "Manhole covers are round because it's easier to dig a round hole than a square one."

☞ "Manhole covers are round because they require less work when being placed over the hole. You don't have to rotate it to make it fit."

☞ "Manhole covers are round because they are cheaper to manufacture since they require less metal than other shapes."

☞ "Manhole covers are round because they are circular."

To give an example of some really unique ideas, during a 2000 speech at Microsoft, Andrei Codrescu was asked the manhole cover question. His response was, "That's easy. In a fight, a round shield is better than a square one. The circle is also a symbol of infinity, which is why church domes are also round. The principle of 'as above as below' reminds pedestrians that they live in a divine world."

Your answer: _____

_____

_____

_____

_____

There are many laws and regulations that protect you from being asked interview questions that would set you up for discrimination. Title VII of the 1964 Civil Rights Act bars discrimination on the basis of race, color, religion, sex, or national origin. The Age Discrimination in Employment Act of 1967 prohibits discrimination against a person 40 or over in any area of employment because of age. Several equal employment opportunity actions protect the handicapped from discrimination, including the Vocational Rehabilitation Act of 1973, Pregnancy Discrimination Act of 1978, and the Americans with Disabilities Act of 1990.

Most HR professionals know which questions are legal and which aren't, but not all interviewers are HR professionals. A hiring manager may not have been trained not to ask these questions. Therefore, you need to be prepared to answer them in a way that can help you get the job without violating your sensibilities. Rather than being offended by the question or simply refusing to answer it, think about what you believe to be the interviewer's concerns. Is he worried about your ability to get along well with a younger or an older workforce? Is she concerned about your family obligations and support for working? Maybe a workforce lacking in ethnic or racial diversity will have to make some adjustments and he wants to know if you are able to assist with those changes in culture? If your health is an obvious concern, she may be asking if you are able to perform the duties of the job for which you are applying. If we believe that present and future behavior is predicted by past behavior, crimes committed in the past may be of concern to your interviewer. The same might be said about financial responsibilities. Regardless of the reason, you want to focus your answer on the concern behind the question while not giving up your legal protections. Avoid embarrassing the interviewer by pointing out that the question is illegal.

188
AGE

☞ **How old are you?**

☞ **When were you born?**

☞ **When did you graduate from high school/college?**

☞ **Aren't you a little young to be seeking a job with this much responsibility?**

☞ **Aren't you a little old for a fast-changing company such as ours?**

☞ **When do you plan to retire?**

☞ **Are you near retirement age?**

While you are protected from being discriminated against because of your age in most cases, there are bona fide occupational qualifications that make it okay to discriminate based on your age. For instance, the FAA sets a ceiling age of 64 for pilots. Actors and actresses who are required to play young parts can't be old. Most states require those who sell alcohol as part of their duties to be 21 years of age or older. The deciding factor is that the qualification must be necessary to normal business operations. The following answers will help you deflect a possibly illegal question without offending the interviewer.

☞ "Although I am young, I have a lot of experience working successfully with people of all ages."

☞ "My extensive experience in this industry can contribute to your company. I enjoy working with people from all generations. I think our different ways of thinking about the world can really help in problem solving and creative elaboration."

Your answer: _____

_____

_____

_____

_____

_____

_____

_____

_____

☞ How many days were you sick last year?

☞ Do you have a heart problem?

☞ You are limping. Did you hurt yourself?

☞ Are you physically fit?

☞ How is your health?

☞ Have you ever been denied health coverage?

☞ Are you handicapped? Do you have any disabilities?

☞ Have you ever filed for workers' compensation?

☞ Have you ever been injured on the job?

189
HEALTH

☞ Do you have a back problem?

☞ How much do you weigh?

☞ When was the last time you saw a doctor?

☞ Do you take prescription medications?

☞ How much money do you spend on prescription drugs?

☞ Have you ever been denied health (or life) insurance?

☞ When was the last time you were in the hospital?

☞ Do you see a doctor regularly?

☞ How many surgeries have you had?

☞ When was the last time you had a physical exam?

☞ Have you ever been treated for a mental health problem?

☞ **Have you ever been treated for substance abuse/drug addiction?**

☞ **Did you get stuck with a lot of medical bills last year?**

☞ **You need to complete this medical history before we can consider you.**

Do not answer these questions directly. These are illegal questions that violate the Americans with Disabilities Act (ADA). You can respond to the first question with something like this:

☞ "I'm not sure. I would have to check my Palm Pilot from last year and get back with you on that."

According to the ADA, if you have an obvious disability—like you are in a wheelchair—the employer has the right to ask you whether you will need accommodations to do the job if they hire you. The employer, however, cannot ask about the nature of your disability, and you are under no obligation to reveal anything about the status of your health to a potential employer. You are always better off not answering health-related questions during an interview.

"Will you be willing to undergo a medical exam if we make you a job offer?" This health-related question may seem illegal at first glance, but it is legal to ask this question, provided the company requires a medical exam of all people offered jobs. It becomes an illegal question when the interviewer asks, **"How do you feel about that?"**

Your answer: _____

_____

_____

_____

190
MARITAL STATUS

☞ **Are you single, married, separated, or divorced?**

☞ **What's your marital status?**

☞ **Do you live with your parents or alone?**

☞ **Does your spouse support your decision to work?**

☞ **Will your spouse mind the long hours you will be working here?**

☞ **Will your family be okay with the frequent travel required on this job?**

☞ **Are you a single parent?**

☞ **Do you have any children?**

☞ **Are you planning to have children?**

☞ **What are your child care arrangements?**

☞ **Have you ever been married before?**

☞ **How do you want to be addressed: Mrs. or Miss?**

☞ **Who is the boss in your family?**

☞ **Is your spouse employed? Will the fact that both of you work be a problem?**

Although Title VII protects a person based on their sex (male/female), it doesn't specifically speak to marital status per se. Some states have set up laws especially to cover marital status. Even if it these questions are not strictly illegal, they have often been interpreted as sexual discrimination by the courts, so you should answer them carefully.

☞ "I wonder if you are concerned about my ability to make a commitment to my work here, show up regularly, and work long hours on occasion. I assure you that I understand the requirements of your job and my work history will support my ability to make the commitment you require."

Your answer: _____

_____

_____

_____

_____

_____

191
RACE/ETHNICITY

☞ **What is your nationality/race?**

☞ **Where were you born?**

☞ **That's a _____ (Greek, Italian, Spanish) surname, isn't it?**

☞ **What language do you speak at home?**

☞ **Where were your parents born?**

☞ **What kind of accent is that?**

☞ **Have you served in the military of countries other than the United States?**

☞ **Can you read English well enough to take this test?**

Race/ethnicity is clearly protected by Title VII, so any of these questions are illegal. It is okay for an employer to ask, "Are you authorized to work in the United States?" and "Are you a U.S. citizen?" provided the question is asked of all applicants. There are rare occasions when ethnicity is a bona fide occupation qualification. If a translation business needs native Spanish speakers, then it is okay to "discriminate."

☞ "Although I grew up in the United States, I have had the advantage of a multicultural experience. I am bilingual and understand the importance of considering culture in my relationships with customers."

☞ "I was born in Eastern Europe and moved to the United States when I was twelve. While my English is excellent, I also speak Russian. My experiences make it easy for me to get along well with a wide variety of people. I am always interested in how others grew up and I'm a good listener."

Your answer: _____

_____

_____

_____

_____

_____

_____

_____

192

CRITE

☞ **Have you ever been arrested?**

☞ **Have you ever committed a crime?**

☞ **Have you ever pled guilty to a crime?**

☞ **Have you ever been in jail?**

The questions asked here are illegal. There is only one legal question and that is, "Have you ever been convicted of a felony?" There is a big difference between committed and convicted. **Convicted** means that you have been tried and found guilty, or that you have pled guilty or no contest to a crime. You do not have to—and should not—answer any other questions about crimes. Instead, turn the question around on the interview and say something like the first example on the back of this card.

☞ "If you are asking if I've ever been convicted of a crime, then the answer is no, I have not."

If you have a felony conviction in your background, you will want to be truthful. Spend as little time as possible on the actual felony—the "what" and "why" may be important to you but that discussion will place the emphasis in your interview in the wrong place. Spend your time talking instead about what is different for you now, about the productive and positive things you have done since your felony. Concentrate on your positives.

☞ "As a young adult, I did some stupid things. I allowed myself to be talked into stealing a car with a rebel friend I had made after moving to a new high school. We were caught, of course, and arrested. I took responsibility for my actions, was convicted of a felony, spent the next two years on probation, and made restitution. I really learned my lesson. I have had no legal difficulties since then, and my judgment with regard to friends really improved!"

Your answer: _____

RELIGION

- ☞ **Are you (Jewish, Christian, Buddhist, ...)?**

- ☞ **Are you a member of any religious group?**

- ☞ **What church do you belong to?**

- ☞ **Do your children go to (Sunday school, church, synagogue, ...)?**

- ☞ **Will your religion keep you from working on weekends?**

- ☞ **Do you sing in the church choir?**

- ☞ **What organizations do you belong to?** (sometimes a legal question)

- ☞ **Is there a religious reason why you didn't shake my hand?**

Religion is definitely a protected class under Title VII of the Civil Rights Act of 1964, and a company must reasonably accommodate your religious practices. An interviewer cannot ask you about your religion (unless your religion is a bona fide occupational qualification for the job—a minister, for instance), and you don't want to answer questions that could set you up for discrimination.

☞ "I consider religion a very personal thing and would prefer not to answer this question."

☞ "I can assure you that my religious practices won't interfere with my work in any way."

The question about your organizational affiliations can be legal if the interviewer is referring to professional or community service organizations and not religious ones. If this question arises in an interview, do not mention your religious affiliations or you will set yourself up for discrimination based on your faith.

Your answer: _____

_____

_____

_____

_____

_____

_____

_____

_____